The
Ontario
Seasonal
Cookbook

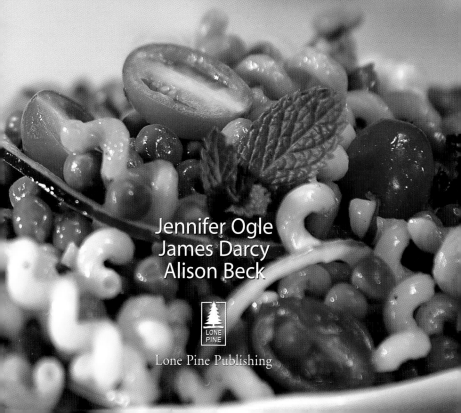

Jennifer Ogle
James Darcy
Alison Beck

LONE
PINE

Lone Pine Publishing

The Publisher: Lone Pine Publishing
10145–81 Avenue
Edmonton, AB, Canada T6E 1W9
Website: www.lonepinepublishing.com

Library and Archives Canada Cataloguing in Publication
Ogle, Jennifer, 1972-
    The Ontario seasonal cookbook / Jennifer Ogle, James Darcy.

Includes index.
ISBN–13: 978-1-55105-582-4
ISBN–10: 1-55105-582-1

    1. Cookery, Canadian--Ontario style. I. Title.

TX715.6.O4525 2007   641.59713   C2007-900026-6

Editorial Director: Nancy Foulds
Editorial: Carol Woo, Sandra Bit
Production Manager: Gene Longson
Book Design and Layout: Willa Kung, Elliot Engley
Cover Design: Gerry Dotto

Photography: All photographs by Nanette Samol, except p. 30, 42, 50, 142 by Merle Prosofsky.
Food Stylist: Jennifer Ogle

A sincere and warm thank you to Nanette, Carol, Nancy, Sandra and Ali—without them this book would not have been possible.

Thank you to the following people who assisted with our photo shoots:
Alison Beck, Laura Peters, Lori Holowaychuk, Mary Lobay, Randy von Beiker

We acknowledge the financial support of the Government of Canada through the Book Publishing Industry Development Program (BPIDP) for our publishing activities.

PC: P14

CONTENTS

DEDICATION

Thank you to seasonal farmers and artisanal producers everywhere
for making food such a joy.

INTRODUCTION

Ontario has the climate and conditions to produce an abundance of food. Our local farms produce meats, eggs, vegetables, fruits and grains. Artisans and small producers offer almost every imaginable food, from cheese, beer, wine and bread to preserves, ice cream and pies, all made from locally grown ingredients. The natural environment is also a rich food source. Walleye, perch, pike and bass swim in our lakes, rivers and streams; wild raspberries, blueberries and strawberries grow in our woodlands; wild mushrooms, fiddlehead ferns and wild rice are there for the picking by anyone who knows where to find them.

Food is a vital part of history and culture. It reflects a place and the people who live there. Ontario's food producers have a rich history that ties their origins with their present places to create a unique and diverse culture. People from all over the world have settled in Ontario and brought their traditional foods with them.

In the past, if a food wasn't in season, we probably couldn't get it. The foods we ate changed depending on the time of the year, and we had an intimate connection with our food and where it came from. Now fresh food can quickly travel from around the world to our dinner tables. Almost any food we may want can be had for a price at just about any time of the year. This selection and convenience are the great advantages of our modern world.

The great disadvantage is that we have become disconnected from where our food comes from. We give little thought to how far it has had to travel and what financial, ethical or environmental costs the production of imported food may have. We may not consider where it was grown, what fertilizer and pesticide regulations a country may or may not have and what residues may remain in our food.

Eating seasonally takes advantage of what locally grown foods are available. It supports the local economy, and it often provides us with fresher and tastier food. Perhaps most importantly, it connects us to the origins of our food. By speaking directly to food producers at such places as farmers' markets, U-pick farms and world-renowned wineries, we learn not only the bounty of foods available at home, but the value of the people involved in their production. We can even become food producers ourselves, by growing our own fruits or vegetables in our gardens or balcony planters.

With this book, we have created a resource of recipes that represent some of the best of what Ontario has to offer. Meat, fowl, eggs, cheese and wine are available all year and can be combined with seasonal foods that change throughout the year. Spring offers us tender asparagus, buttery spinach and sweet, crisp peas. Summer brings many fresh fruits, wonderful to enjoy in pies, ice cream and smoothies. Fall's first frost sweetens cabbage, broccoli and kale. Winter warming comes in the form of roasted root vegetables and soups. It's all here, in the appetizers, salads, soups, main and side dishes, desserts and snacks that make up the seasons of this book.

About the Author

Canadian chef Jennifer Ogle learned her craft from a variety of sources, among them the renowned French cooking school *La Varenne,* which lead to an opportunity to work in the Michelin-starred restaurant *La Madeleine* in Burgundy, France.

Jennifer recalls that her love of cooking started at an early age, when many Sunday afternoons were spent experimenting in the kitchen. Today, Jennifer enjoys all aspects of the culinary world, from cooking to writing, with a particular passion for seasonal, local ingredients.

In Our Kitchen

We have found the following ingredient choices and cooking procedures to be successful in our kitchen and recommend them highly wherever possible.

Butter is unsalted and is easiest to measure using the convenient markings on the wrapping.

Citrus juices are fresh squeezed.

Eggs are large, free-run eggs. They should be at room temperature for baking.

Flour is unbleached all-purpose.

Herbs are fresh, unless stated otherwise. In a pinch, the best alternative to fresh is frozen, not dried. You can freeze herbs yourself in the summer when they are plentiful, and you can even find them in the freezer section of some of the better grocery stores.

Mushrooms, such as morels and chanterelles, can be found in the wild, but we advise that you confirm the identification of mushrooms with an experienced collector before cooking them; some species of mushrooms are acutely toxic and can cause death.

Stocks are homemade. Good quality stocks available in tetra packs are the best substitute. Avoid using those nasty little cubes. Miso, a fermented soybean paste, is another interesting alternative to stock, and it will keep in the refrigerator for several months. Stir it in 1 Tbsp (15 mL) at a time until you have a rich, full flavour.

Sugar is organic and unrefined rather than white and bleached. When looking for a rich brown sugar, use muscovado sugar, available in grocery and health food stores. It still contains the minerals and vitamins originally in the sugar cane plant, and it has a full molasses flavour.

Yeast is regular dry yeast; ½ oz (15 g) dry yeast is equal to 1 Tbsp fresh yeast.

Essential Ingredients

The following ingredients are used in many of the recipes in this book; special ingredients found in just one or two recipes are described where they are used. Some items are widely available, whereas others are best sought in gourmet, specialty food, health food or ethnic stores or obtained by mail order or the Internet.

Bay Leaves— Fresh leaves have such a different flavour that they are worth the effort to find. They are occasionally available at large grocery stores and can be specially ordered. In a well-sealed container in the fridge, they can last three or four months.

Coconut Milk—Use unsweetened coconut milk in cans. Naturally sweet, it is often better than cream in savory dishes.

Garlic—Use fresh garlic! An Italian friend once told me that if you can't be bothered to peel and chop fresh garlic you shouldn't be allowed to use it!

Lemons and Limes—Use fresh! You can't compare the taste to concentrate.

Mayonnaise—It's always better homemade:

5 egg yolks

⅔ cup (150 mL) extra virgin olive oil

¼ cup (60 mL) good quality vinegar or juice of 1 lemon

pinch of sea salt to taste

- You need both hands free to make mayonnaise. Spread a damp cloth on your counter, nestle a medium-sized bowl in its centre and wrap it around base of bowl to keep it steady while you whisk.

- Whisk yolk, vinegar and salt in bowl until well combined and yolk has lightened in colour.

- Add oil, a drop at a time, whisking continuously until mixture emulsifies and thickens.

- When about half of oil has been added, add remaining oil in a slow, steady stream. Store, covered, in refrigerator for up to 5 days. You can thin your mayonnaise by lightly whisking in some water.

- Many people like to add mustard or fresh herbs to their mayonnaise. Adding minced garlic turns plain mayonnaise into aioli. Makes just over 1 cup (250 mL).

Mustard—Use good quality mustard for everything from sandwiches to dressings to sauces. When you are down to the last few teaspoons clinging to the bottom of your mustard jar, add fresh lemon juice, olive oil, sea salt and fresh pepper for a yummy impromptu salad dressing. Just shake and enjoy.

Oil, Sesame—Use for a nutty flavour addition. Store it in the fridge.

Oil, Olive—Extra virgin olive oil is indispensable. Try olive oil from Italy, Spain or Greece.

Oil, Grape Seed—Use for higher heat cooking.

Pepper, Fresh—Please don't use pre-ground pepper; it has such poor flavour. A variety of peppercorns are available. Black or white can be used interchangeably in any of the recipes.

Salt—Great salt is the key to great cooking. Salt brings out the flavour in food. Sea salt, kosher salt, Celtic salt—choose a favourite. Better yet, obtain some of each. Using a better quality salt also means that you will use less, because the flavour is more intense. If you need to reduce salt even further for health reasons, use fresh herbs, various spices and flavour lifters, such as lemon juice, to maintain the flavour intensity while reducing the salt content.

Soy Sauce—Both tamari and shoyu are high quality, fermented and chemical-free "soy sauces" that are used to enhance flavour and impart a unique saltiness.

Star Anise—This strongly anise-scented Oriental spice is commonly sold dried, as quarter-sized, star-shaped clusters of 5 to 10 pods, each containing a single seed. The seeds can be used on their own, crushed or ground, or the entire stars can be added, then removed.

Vinegar, Apple Cider—Use when you need an all-purpose vinegar; organic, unrefined and unpasteurized has the best flavour.

Vinegar, Balsamic—Its unique flavour is great in everything from soups to sweets. Be sure to try authentic balsamic from Modena, Italy.

Measuring

Dry ingredients should be spooned into the measuring cup and leveled off with a knife or spatula.

Measurements are in both metric and imperial. Note that for butter, a pound is considered to be 454 g; for meat, vegetables, etc., a pound is 500 g.

Solids, including butter and most cheeses, are measured in dry-measure cups and liquids in liquid-measure cups.

Spring Heirloom Tomato Salad

Serves 4

If you are interested in tomatoes—those tomatoes reminiscent of days in the garden as a child picking the sun-warmed fruit right off the vine—then look no further than Leamington, the Tomato Capital of Canada. With North America's largest concentration of greenhouses, Leamington is tomato heaven. People there hold a tomato festival the third week in August. Leamington also sports the world's largest tomato sculpture and the Heinz ketchup factory, which produces most of the country's ketchup. Native to the Americas, tomatoes (*Solanum lycopersicum*) arrived in Europe in the 16th century. Although Europeans initially admired tomatoes for their beauty, they believed the entire plant to be poisonous. The leaves and stems do indeed contain toxic compounds, but the fruits are quite edible.

1 clove garlic, minced

splash of white balsamic vinegar (see Essential Ingredients, p. 6)

¼ cup (60 mL) olive oil

sea salt and freshly ground pepper to taste

1 lb (500 g) heirloom tomatoes, washed, cored and sliced ½ in (1 cm) thick

½ lb (250 g) bocconcini, sliced the same thickness as the tomatoes

handful of fresh basil leaves, washed and patted dry

French baguette

In a salad bowl, add the garlic, vinegar and oil. Then add the tomatoes, tossing gently to coat with dressing. Season to taste with salt and pepper.

On individual plates, layer tomato slices with bocconcini and some basil tucked in between and around the tomato slices. Scatter remaining basil leaves on top and drizzle remaining dressing.

Serve with slices of crusty French baguette.

Tip
Fresh tomatoes from the garden or the farmers' market would also work in this recipe.

Bocconcini are a form of semi-ripe mozzarella cheese that comes in small, soft, white balls.

Wyndym Farms in Niagara is a family-owned farm dedicated to growing specialty vegetables such as heirloom tomatoes, which can be found at high-end restaurants and, in season, at the farm gate.

Asparagus and Chèvre Salad

Serves 4

Ontario, like many provinces in Canada, is dotted with artisan goat cheese producers. Over 30 percent of the country's goat farms are located in Ontario; of the 2.21 million gallons (10 million litres) of goat's milk processed yearly, over half goes towards cheese making. *Chèvre* is the French word for "goat," and it has become synonymous with the French-style, tangy, fluffy, soft cheese made from goat's milk. Most grocery-store varieties are mild, moist and creamy and come in logs or cylinders, sometimes rolled in herbs or spices such as peppercorns or coated with ash or edible leaves. Goat's milk can also be made into other types of cheese, including feta, Gouda and Brie.

1 bunch (about 2 lb [1 kg]) asparagus, trimmed

splash of olive oil

sea salt and freshly ground pepper to taste

1 lb (500 g) package frozen peas, refreshed in boiling water, drained and cooled

1 cup (250 g) chèvre, crumbled

½ cup (125 mL) fresh mint, chopped

½ cup (125 mL) fresh basil, chopped

1 lime cut into 4 wedges

Preheat barbecue to medium-high heat. Toss trimmed asparagus with olive oil, salt and pepper. Grill for 4 minutes, turning once. Set aside.

In a bowl, toss together the remaining ingredients, except the lime. Cut the warm asparagus into bite-sized pieces and add to the bowl, toss and season again if needed. (You cut the asparagus after because it is much easier to grill if left whole!) Divide among 4 plates and garnish each salad with a lime wedge.

Tip

Soft cheeses such as chèvre do not slice well—they often end up as a crumbled mess, half stuck to the knife. The easiest way to cut soft cheese is with taut dental floss. Just be sure to use unflavoured floss!

Tip
Allow cheese to come to room temperature for at least 30 minutes (longer for hard cheese or if the room is particularly cold) before serving in order to enjoy its full flavour and aroma. Portion cheese, if desired, while cold and keep it wrapped so it doesn't dry out before you are ready to serve.

Lobster Cocktail

Serves 6

Spring marks the start of lobster season, and spring lobsters are regarded as the best quality because of their thick shells, high meat content and excellent taste. Lobsters used to be considered food for the poor or fertilizer for the garden, but they soon began to be appeal to sophisticated palates. Today, modern transportation methods ensure that fresh, live lobster can be shipped from the Maritimes to Ontario overnight. Lobster can be served in various ways, from homey chowders and rolls to fancy dishes such as Lobster Thermidor and Lobster Newburg. In this recipe, it's paired with horseradish for a tasty, refreshing treat.

1 x 8 oz (250 g) lobster, fresh or frozen (thawed and squeezed of excess liquid)

3 Tbsp (45 mL) mayonnaise

1 tsp (5 mL) mustard

1 Tbsp (15 mL) fresh mint, chopped

1 Tbsp (15 mL) fresh tarragon, chopped

½ tsp (2 mL) lime zest

½ tsp (2 mL) orange zest

juice of ½ lime

1 tsp (5 mL) horseradish, or more to taste

1 Tbsp (15 mL) capers, squeezed dry and chopped

⅓ cup (75 mL) roasted red bell pepper, diced small

sea salt and freshly ground pepper to taste

Mix lobster, mayonnaise and the rest of ingredients, except for avocado, and season with salt and pepper. In a separate bowl, toss avocado cubes in lime juice. To serve, layer the lobster with the avocado. Garnish with green onions or caviar and serve as an appetizer with your favourite crackers. Makes approximately 3 cups (750 mL).

Spicy horseradish—the aroma alone is enough to make a grown man cry—is the root of a perennial herb native to Europe and Asia.

Now naturalized in North America, horseradish (Armoracia rusticana) can be very difficult to eradicate once planted in your garden. It is available, starting in late spring, at your local farmers' market.

Avocado Mix
1 avocado, peeled and
cubed into small dice
juice of ½ lime

Garnish
green onions, sliced
or caviar

Fresh Pea and Mint Pasta Salad

Serves 4 to 6

Peas *(Pisum sativum)* are a member of the legume family of plants, which also includes beans, lentils and peanuts. Peas are a cool-climate crop that do best in moderate summer temperatures. They mature about 60 days after planting, come into season in June and are available at local farmers' markets, U-pick farms and some grocery stores. If you grow them yourself, a second crop can be planted in August to ripen in the cooler days of fall. Peas were first cultivated about 7000 BC, shortly after wheat, and were important as a source of food that could be dried and stored for long periods of time. In fact, it wasn't until around the 1600s that it became fashionable to eat peas fresh off the vine. Pea pods are also edible, although it is most common to eat cultivars such as mangetout and sugar snap peas that have been specifically bred to be eaten in their entirety.

1 x 12 oz (340 g) package pasta, cooked and cooled (see Tip)

1 cup (250 mL) cherry tomatoes, halved

½ small red onion, halved and very thinly sliced

2 cups (500 mL) fresh peas

2 Tbsp (30 mL) fresh mint, finely chopped

1 Tbsp (15 mL) fresh oregano, finely chopped

1 cup (250 mL) chopped roasted chicken (optional)

In a large bowl, gently toss the pasta, tomatoes, onion, peas, mint, oregano and chicken, if using. In a small bowl, whisk the dressing ingredients together, pour over the salad and toss again. Serve immediately, or store, covered, in the refrigerator until ready to serve as a side dish.

Tip
Pastas such as gemelli, fusilli, rotini or radiatore are perfect for pasta salads because their texture holds the dressing nicely.

Dressing

2 Tbsp (30 mL) white wine vinegar

¼ cup (60 mL) olive oil

½ tsp (2 mL) Dijon mustard

3 Tbsp (45 mL) mayonnaise

sea salt and freshly ground pepper to taste

Cipollini and Asiago Stuffed Morels

Serves 4 as an appetizer

Highly prized for their meaty, mushroomy flavour, morels *(Morchella)* are edible cup fungi. May is morel month in Ontario, where, if luck is on your side, you could end up feasting after an enjoyable day of foraging. Many species of morel are found here, but the two most common and easily identifiable are the yellow morel *(M. esculenta)* and the black morel *(M. elata)*. Beware the false morel *(Gyromitra esculenta)*! A cousin to the morel and similar in appearance, this poisonous mushroom will fool novice hunters. Morels generally grow year after year on forested sites, preferring the company of ash trees, but they flourish in the years immediately following a forest fire. If you're interested in foraging, pick up a copy of George Barron's *Mushrooms of Ontario and Eastern Canada*.

1 Tbsp (15 mL) grape seed or canola oil

½ cup (125 mL) cipollini onion, peeled and quartered

1 lb (500 g) fresh morels, reserve 12 of the largest ones to stuff and chop the rest for stuffing

¼ cup (60 mL) white wine

1 clove garlic, minced

¼ cup (60 mL) parsley, chopped

2 Tbsp (30 mL) chives, chopped

¼ cup (60 mL) grated Asiago cheese

2 to 3 Tbsp (30 to 45 mL) panko

sea salt and freshly ground pepper to taste

In a medium saucepan, heat the oil over medium heat and sauté the cipollini onions until they start to caramelize, about 5 minutes. Add the chopped mushrooms, white wine and cook for about 5 minutes. Add garlic, cook for 2 to 3 minutes and remove pan from heat. Stir in remaining ingredients, except for the 12 reserved morels. Stuff the reserved mushrooms with the filling.

For the lime mayonnaise, stir together lime zest and mayonnaise. Set aside.

For breading, place flour, eggs and panko into separate bowls. Heat clarified butter in a saucepan over medium-high heat.

Bread the stuffed morels one at a time, dipping first in the flour, then the egg and finally the panko. Cook the mushrooms in the butter until brown and crispy. Serve hot with lime mayonnaise.

Tip
To remove any unwanted critters hiding in the morels, soak mushrooms in salted water for at least 1 hour.

Tip
To make clarified butter, melt unsalted butter slowly over low heat. Gradually, froth will rise to the top with a layer of clear golden oil in the middle and a layer of milk solids on the bottom. Clarified butter is the middle layer. Skim off the froth and carefully ladle out the clear oil, leaving out the milk solids.

Lime Mayonnaise
zest from 1 lime
½ cup (125 mL) mayonnaise (see Essential Ingredients, p. 6)

Breading
½ cup (125 mL) flour
3 eggs, lightly beaten
2 cups (500 mL) panko
1 cup (250 mL) clarified butter

Spring Lamb Tagine with Preserved Lemons and Olives

Serves 6

One of the meatiest and tastiest breeds of sheep, the Charollais is a relative newcomer to the Canadian sheep industry. The Charollais breed originated in the Saône-et-Loire region of France. In 1994 Land's End farm in Belwood, Ontario was one of only four farms in the province to embryo transfer the Charollais breed into its flock. Since then, high demand for this exceptional breed has led to the sale of stock to farms elsewhere in Ontario and in Alberta, Quebec and Prince Edward Island. Land's End farm sells its lamb off the farm in June, July and December. It is believed that sheep were domesticated by 8900 BC, in locations known today as Iraq and Romania. Some of the oldest recipes for lamb come from Greece, where lamb is still a favourite.

olive oil, about ¼ cup (60 mL)

1½ lbs (750 g) lamb shoulder meat, cubed

1 yellow onion, diced

2 cups (500 mL) lamb stock (see next page)

2 large ripe tomatoes, chopped

1 small turnip, peeled and cubed

2 carrots, peeled and sliced

½ preserved lemon (p. 154), finely chopped

2 cups (500 mL) Cerignola olives, or other unpitted green olives

⅓ cup (75 mL) dried apricots, sliced

1 bunch cilantro, chopped, some reserved for garnish

¼ cup (60 mL) parsley, chopped

1 clove garlic, minced

1 tsp (5 mL) cinnamon

1 tsp (5 mL) coriander

harissa to taste

sea salt and freshly ground pepper to taste

Preheat oven to 325° F (160° C). Heat a splash of olive oil in a large ovenproof pot and brown the lamb in small batches, adding more oil if necessary. Add onion and sauté for 5 minutes. Combine remaining ingredients and bring to a boil. Cover and bake in oven for about 2 hours until meat is tender. Serve with couscous.

Couscous

Bring stock or water with oil in a small saucepan to a gentle boil. Stir in couscous. Remove from heat and leave it covered for 5 minutes. Fluff with a fork before serving. Makes about 3 cups (750 mL).

Lamb Stock

Cover lamb bones with cold water and bring to a boil. Reduce to a simmer and skim off the froth as it rises to the surface. Add the rest of ingredients and simmer for about 2 hours. Strain through a fine sieve and cool. Refrigerate overnight and remove the layer of fat on the surface.

Stock will keep for 4 days refrigerated or 2 months frozen. Makes about 5 cups (1.25 L).

Couscous

1¼ cups (310 mL) stock or water

1 Tbsp (15 mL) canola oil

1¼ cups (310 mL) couscous

Lamb Stock

1 lb (500 g) lamb bones

8 cups (2 L) water

1 yellow onion, peeled and sliced in half

1 carrot, peeled and cut in chunks

1 parsnip, peeled and cut in chunks

½ cup (125 mL) celery, cut in chunks

1 tsp (5 mL) black peppercorns

1 clove garlic

Broccoli and Tempeh Rice Bowl

Serves 4

In Ontario, fresh broccoli first becomes available in June and, weather permitting, can last through the first two weeks of October. A member of the cabbage family, broccoli (*Brassica oleracea*) is a very close relative of cauliflower. It was loved in what is now Tuscany long before it was eaten anywhere else, and it was adopted by the Romans when they invaded the region. When it first came to Britain, broccoli was called "Italian asparagus." Broccoli makes the grade as a popular "superfood" because it is loaded with vitamins and the anti-cancer enzyme sulforaphane.

2 Tbsp (30 mL) soy sauce

1 Tbsp (30 mL) mirin or sweet rice wine

2 Tbsp (30 mL) light miso

1 tsp (5 mL) toasted sesame oil

¼ tsp (1 mL) cornstarch

2 tsp (10 mL) grape seed or canola oil

1 Tbsp (15 mL) ginger, finely chopped

2 tsp (10 mL) lemongrass, tender bottom part only, chopped

2 garlic cloves, minced

1 package Indonesian-style tempeh, cut into ½-inch strips

1 head of broccoli, cut into florets

½ cup (125 mL) each yellow and red pepper, cut into strips

½ cup (125 mL) snow peas

½ cup (125 mL) green onions, cut in ¼-inch diagonal strips

2 tsp (10 mL) black sesame seeds

½ tsp (2 mL) sea salt

2 cups (500 mL) hot, cooked brown rice

In a small bowl, combine soy sauce, mirin, miso, sesame oil and cornstarch. Stir with a whisk and set aside. Heat oil in a large skillet over medium-high heat and sauté ginger, lemongrass and garlic for 1 minute or just until mixture begins to brown. Add tempeh and sauté for 2 minutes, then add broccoli, peppers, snow peas and sauté for 1 minute. Add reserved mixture to skillet and cook for 1 minute, until sauce has slightly thickened. Remove from heat and stir in green onions, sesame seeds and salt. Serve over rice.

Tip
Soak your broccoli in warm, salted water to get rid of any critters. As with all members of the cabbage family, broccoli is best used within a few days of picking to retain its sweet flavour and mild odour.

Tempeh is a fermented soybean product that has been enjoyed in Southeast Asia for centuries. It is fermented with a Rhizopus mould, which makes the soy protein more easily digestible. Tempeh has a deep, nutty flavour and can be used in meals as a substitute for tofu or meat. Here in Ontario, it is available at most supermarkets.

Gnocchi in a Sorrel Sauce

Serves 2 as a main course, 4 as a side dish

Sorrel *(Rumex acetosa)* is a perennial herb with a sharp, thirst-quenching, lemony flavour. Not yet widely popular in Ontario, sorrel is perfectly suited to our climate, is frost tolerant and is an excellent addition to anyone's garden. Sorrel comes up early in spring and can be enjoyed through to autumn. To keep leaves tender and mild, pinch off flowers as they come up. Sorrel grows wild throughout the province; you may already be weeding it out of your garden. It is also available at local farmers' markets and occasionally in the herb section of large grocery stores. Sorrel can be used in anything from soups to salads and stews, and it can be minced and frozen for winter use. It is a staple in the cuisine of central Europe, where it is cultivated as a vegetable. Sorrel most often appears in a soup enriched with egg and sour cream, which is believed to share the same culinary history as borscht.

1 lb (500 g) package gnocchi

splash of olive oil

1 Tbsp (15 mL) unsalted butter

1 small shallot, minced

½ cup (125 mL) white wine

1 cup (250 mL) heavy cream (32%)

1 packed cup (250 g) sorrel, chopped

¼ cup (60 mL) parsley, chopped

sea salt and freshly ground pepper to taste

good sized pinch of fresh chives, chopped

handful of fresh grated Parmesan cheese

Bring a big pot of salted water to a rolling boil and cook the gnocchi until they float to the surface. Drain, toss with a splash of olive oil and set aside.

In a large saucepan, heat the butter and add the shallot and cook for 2 to 3 minutes, then add the white wine and cook until the wine has reduced by half. Add the cream and continue cooking for 5 minutes at medium-high heat.

Purée sorrel and parsley in a blender along with hot cream mixture until everything is incorporated; the sauce turns a jade green colour. Pour sauce back into pan along with the gnocchi just to heat through and season with salt and pepper. Serve in warm bowls with chives and Parmesan cheese sprinkled on top.

"Gnocchi" is Italian for "dumplings"; the singular, "gnocco," means "lump." Gnocchi are often made using potatoes, but they can also be made with durum wheat, flour or ricotta cheese. Traditionally, gnocchi are served with tomato sauce or melted butter and Parmesan cheese, but they lend themselves well to almost any sauce.

Herb Pesto

Makes about 2 cups (500 mL)

Basil *(Ocimum basilicum)* enjoys the warm days of summer in Ontario. It can be grown indoors or out, but it does not tolerate the slightest bit of cold, so basil should only be moved outside once it is warm and the chance of a late frost has passed. Indoors, basil prefers a south-facing window. Basil will grow abundantly if it is kept in a humid environment with moist soil, conditions easily met in Ontario. Basil is thought to have originated in India, where it was considered a holy plant and was often planted near shrines and temples. Legend has it that the Greeks named the plant βασιλευς, meaning "king," when it was found growing above the spot where the Holy Cross was rediscovered in the 4th century AD. Even today, basil is considered the high priest of herbs. There are dozens of varieties of this herb, from licorice and cinnamon-flavoured basil to purple varieties and spicy warm ones, such as Thai basil.

4 cups (32 oz) fresh basil leaves, rinsed, patted dry and well packed

4 cloves garlic, peeled

1 cup (250 mL) pine nuts or other nut of your choice

1½ cups (375 mL) freshly grated Parmesan or Pecorino cheese

1½ cups (375 mL) extra virgin olive oil

sea salt and freshly ground pepper to taste

In a blender, pulse basil and garlic until well crushed. Add nuts, process to crush, then add cheese. You should have a thick paste. Slowly drizzle in olive oil, continuously mixing. Adjust seasoning and serve with pasta or vegetables, or add to a soup, etc.

Tip
Traditionally, pesto is made in a mortar and pestle. A food processor also works just fine—the method is the same.

Variation
Genoa, Italy, is the birthplace of pesto, where it is traditionally made with basil and pine nuts. For variety, try other herbs, such as arugula, cilantro or even cooked artichokes, or nuts and seeds, such as walnuts and sunflower kernels.

Richters Herbs of Goodwood, Ontario, is one of the largest herb nurseries in North America and sells over 40 selections of basil, along with just about every other herb you can imagine. You can visit their nursery or order their plants and seeds by mail.

Potato Frittata

Serves 4

Potatoes are the number one fresh vegetable crop in Ontario. The late potato breeder Gary Johnston developed the much-loved Yukon Gold potato during the 1960s at the University of Guelph. The first Canadian potato to be sold by name, it took over 13 years to develop. It's hard to believe, but the average Canadian eats about 163 pounds (74 kilograms) of potatoes per year! With more than 150 seed varieties, potatoes are the most eaten vegetable, accounting for more than 63 percent of total vegetable sales in the country. From the Italian word *fritto* for "fried," a frittata is an open-faced omelette made with cheese and other ingredients mixed into the eggs. It is a classic Roman recipe traditionally served at Easter. Incorporating potatoes into this breakfast makes it an especially satisfying and comforting one-dish meal.

2 Tbsp (30 mL) butter

3 onions, sliced

2 medium Yukon Gold potatoes, peeled, cooked and sliced

8 eggs

¾ cup (175 mL) cream or milk

sea salt and freshly ground black pepper

½ cup (125 mL) aged Cheddar cheese, grated

1 Tbsp (15 mL) fresh thyme, chopped

Preheat broiler to 500° F (260° C). Melt butter in a 9-inch (23 cm) nonstick, ovenproof pan over low heat. Add onions and sauté, stirring occasionally, for 10 to 15 minutes until onions are golden brown. Add potato slices and cook until starting to brown, about 5 minutes. Whisk eggs, cream or milk, salt and pepper in a bowl to combine. Pour egg mixture over onions in frying pan and sprinkle with cheese and thyme. Cook frittata for 5 to 6 minutes or until it is almost set. To finish cooking, place frittata under broiler for 1 minute. Cut into wedges and serve along with your breakfast favourites.

Chefs around the world love the Yukon Gold potato for its texture, flavour and tempting golden flesh.

Braised Swiss Chard

Serves 4

This cool-climate vegetable is ideal for Ontario gardens because it can withstand frost, and, when planted in early spring, is usually ready to eat within four to six weeks. It also rivals spinach as a great leafy green because, unlike spinach, it contains no oxalic acid, allowing the minerals it contains to be more readily digestible. Chard *(Beta vulgaris* var. *cicla;* sometimes known as silverbeet, perpetual spinach or mangold) is a kind of beet grown for its leaves rather than its roots. Chard packs a huge amount of vitamin A and is naturally high in sodium—one cup (250 ml) contains 313 mg. It is indigenous to the Mediterranean, but it is often called "Swiss chard" as a result of its initial scientific description in the 16th century by a Swiss botanist.

2 small red onions, chopped

1 Tbsp (15 mL) butter

2 lbs (1 kg) chard leaves, stems removed

¼ cup (60 mL) white wine

sea salt and freshly ground pepper to taste

Sauté the onions in the butter over medium heat in a large pan until they are nearly softened and lightly browned, about 8 to 10 minutes. Meanwhile, clean chard leaves (see Tip) and slice into ribbons.

Add the chard leaves and wine. Cook rapidly, stirring frequently, until the chard is wilted and the liquid has evaporated, about 5 minutes.

Season with salt and pepper, and serve as a side dish.

Tip
To clean chard, simply swish in cool water and pat dry. The stems and leaves are both edible, but should be cooked separately because the stems take longer to cook.

Chard can be used instead of spinach or kale in your favourite recipes.

Pan-fried Fiddlehead Greens

Serves 4 to 6

Ostrich fern *(Matteuccia struthiopteris)* grows in moist or wet, forested parts of Ontario. This seasonal treat is appreciated equally for the joy of the harvest as it is for the taste. Native peoples, who have harvested fiddleheads for centuries, believe that this food has a cleansing quality, providing a sort of rejuvenation after a long winter. Some people describe the taste of fiddleheads as a cross between green beans and asparagus. You eat only the curled tip of the frond, which resembles the ornamental scroll on the end of a violin. Ostrich fern is also available as an ornamental shade plant at garden centres and can be grown easily in a shady spot in your own garden. Given their tendency to spread, you will be able to supply your own table after only a few short years.

1 lb (500 g) fresh fiddleheads

⅓ cup (75 mL) unsalted butter

juice of ½ lemon

pinch each of sea salt, pepper, paprika

⅓ cup (75 mL) fine breadcrumbs

Clean fiddleheads well and cook in boiling, salted water for 5 to 7 minutes. In a pan, melt butter and add lemon juice, salt, pepper, paprika and breadcrumbs. Toss hot fiddleheads in pan for another 3 to 5 minutes to coat well. Serves 6 as a side dish.

Tip
A great way to clean the papery, brown scales from fiddleheads is to shake them in small batches in a paper bag.

Traditional Steamed Fiddlehead Greens
Prepare fiddleheads by washing them well in several changes of clean water, then steam until tender, about 10 minutes. While still hot, toss with butter and vinegar. Season with salt and pepper.

1 lb (500 g) fresh fiddleheads

¼ cup (60 mL) unsalted butter

2 Tbsp (30 mL) champagne vinegar or cider vinegar

sea salt and pepper to taste

Hot Cross Buns

Makes 12

For many people, Easter wouldn't be the same without the spicy, sweet treat of hot cross buns. Hot cross buns are eaten in many Christian countries on Good Friday, a welcome treat after the long Lenten fast. They are adorned with a cross (often made of pastry or icing), which symbolizes the crucifixion of Christ. The origins of the bun are likely a mixture of Christian and pagan traditions. One famous story recounts that during the Lenten season, England's Queen Elizabeth I attempted to abolish Roman Catholicism along with these buns. When it became evident that the practice of putting crosses on buns could not be stopped, she passed a law that limited consumption of the buns to certain religious ceremonies. Supporters of hot cross buns at the time claimed that the buns would not rise without the cross, leading some culinary historians to believe that the first hot cross buns were scored with a knife, rather than decorated with pastry.

1 Tbsp (15 mL) quick-rise yeast

¼ cup (60 mL) sugar

¼ cup (60 mL) warm water

2 cups (500 mL) unbleached bread flour

⅓ cup (75 mL) stone-ground whole grain bread flour

1 tsp (5 mL) sea salt

½ tsp (2 mL) each dried cinnamon, coriander and lavender

½ tsp (2 mL) freshly grated nutmeg

2 Tbsp (30 mL) cold unsalted butter, diced

⅓ cup (75 mL) currants

¼ cup (60 mL) golden raisins

¼ cup (60 mL) mixed fruit peel, finely chopped

1 large egg, beaten

1 cup (250 ml) milk

Prepare 1 parchment-lined baking sheet.

Put the yeast and 1 Tbsp of sugar in a small bowl with warm water until dissolved. Let sit 10 minutes.

Combine the flours, salt and spices in a bowl. Add the diced butter and rub into the flour using the tips of your fingers until the mixture looks like fine crumbs. Mix in currants, golden raisins and mixed fruit peel, then make a well in the centre of the mixture.

Add the yeast mixture, the remaining sugar and beaten egg to the well and approximately half the milk. Gradually add enough milk to the flour-fruit mixture to make a soft, but not sticky, dough. Add more milk, if necessary, or extra flour, if the dough is too sticky.

Turn the dough onto a lightly floured work surface and knead thoroughly for 10 minutes.

Return the dough to the bowl and then cover the bowl with plastic wrap. Let rise in a warm spot in the kitchen until doubled in size, about 1½ hours.

Punch down the dough a couple of times to deflate and divide it into 12 equal pieces. Shape each into a neat ball and set well apart on the baking sheet. Slip the baking sheet into a large plastic bag and let rise as before until doubled in size, 45 minutes to 1 hour.

Meanwhile, preheat the oven to 400° F (200° C).

To make the dough for the cross pattern, put flour, butter and sugar into a small bowl and rub butter into the flour with the tips of your fingers until the mixture looks like coarse crumbs. Stir in cold water and mix; the dough will be firm. Roll the pastry into a long, thin rope about ⅛ inch (3 mm) thick and cut into segments approximately 3 inches (8 cm) long.

When the buns have risen, uncover and brush with a little water to dampen, then place the cross pattern on top of the buns. Bake for 15 to 20 minutes until golden brown.

Meanwhile, to prepare the glaze, combine honey and milk until smooth. As soon as the buns are done, place them on a cooling rack and brush immediately with the hot glaze. Eat warm or toasted, or freeze for up to 1 month.

It is actually during the hot sticky weather of summer in Ontario that yeast breads rise best. Unfortunately, these are the same days that we are most reluctant to turn our stoves on for baking.

Pastry Cross

⅓ cup (75 mL) white flour

scant ¼ cup (60 mL) cold unsalted butter, diced

2 tsp (10 mL) sugar

1 to 2 Tbsp (15 to 30 mL) cold water

Glaze

3 Tbsp (45 mL) honey

3 Tbsp (45 mL) milk

Asparagus Omelette

Serves 1

Asparagus is one of the sure signs of spring in Ontario. Spears emerge from the ground any time from late April on. Most of the asparagus grown commercially in Ontario is green, but there is also a white variety. Eggs are also associated with spring, rebirth and immortality. In many cultures, Easter eggs are elaborately decorated and given as gifts, the most extravagant being the Fabergé eggs of the Russian tsars. Perhaps the most famous ornamental eggs are the pysanka, which are decorated using a written-wax batik method that dates back to the Trypillian culture and continues to be hugely popular in many central and eastern European countries today. In Ukraine, it is believed that the fate of the world rests on the continuation of the pysanka tradition.

3 eggs, separated

2 Tbsp (30 mL) cream (10 to 18 %)

1 Tbsp (15 mL) unsalted butter

pinch of sea salt and freshly ground pepper

6 thin asparagus stalks, or 3 thick, lightly steamed

2 Tbsp (30 mL) Boursin cheese, herb and garlic or pepper

1 Tbsp (15 mL) fresh chopped chives

In a medium bowl, blend egg yolks and cream with a fork. In another bowl, beat the whites until soft peaks form. Gently fold the whites into the yolks. In a nonstick 10-inch (25 cm) pan, melt butter over medium-high heat. Pour in eggs, swirling around pan to distribute evenly. Season with salt and pepper. Using a spatula, push the eggs gently around to allow the uncooked egg to flow underneath, run the spatula around the sides of the omelette to loosen. When it is almost set, about 40 seconds, lay the asparagus and cheese in the middle of the omelette. Fold one-third of the omelette over the filling, then lift the pan and slide the opposite third onto your plate and fold the omelette onto itself, forming a neat tri-fold package. Sprinkle with chives and serve immediately.

Tip
When buying asparagus, choose firm, bright green stalks for the best flavour.

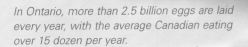

In Ontario, more than 2.5 billion eggs are laid every year, with the average Canadian eating over 15 dozen per year.

Maple Syrup Pie

Serves 6

Sweet and distinctive, maple syrup is synonymous with both spring and Canada. Aboriginal peoples were the first to harvest the sap of maple trees. Each year, they left their winter hunting grounds and moved to mid-altitude maple groves, where they set up sugar camps and collected the sap using buckets made from birch. Jacques Cartier, in the 16th century, was the first to write about the acquisition of maple syrup from North American maple trees. In the early days of European settlement, most maple sap was made into sugar, not syrup. In 1818 maple sugar sold for half the cost of imported cane sugar, and, by 1861 Canada was producing almost 14 million pounds (6.5 million kilograms) of maple sugar annually. Canada currently produces about 85 percent of the world's maple syrup, exporting to more than 30 countries. Although the majority of Canada's maple syrup comes from Quebec, there is a well-respected cottage industry in Ontario.

½ cup (125 mL) maple syrup

1½ cups (375 mL) brown sugar

3 Tbsp (45 mL) flour

1 cup (250 mL) heavy cream (32%)

1 tsp (5 mL) vanilla

1 Tbsp (15 mL) unsalted butter

pinch of salt

pinch of nutmeg (optional)

½ cup (125 mL) chopped nuts such as pecans or walnuts (optional)

pastry, enough for a single crust (see p. 77 or use purchased)

Preheat oven to 350° F (175° C). In a saucepan over low heat, bring maple syrup, brown sugar, flour and cream to a boil and simmer for about 10 minutes or until thickened. Stir in vanilla, butter and salt. Add nutmeg and nuts, if using. Pour into a prepared pie crust and bake for 30 to 35 minutes.

Let cool to room temperature before serving. Serve with fresh fruit and ice cream.

At the 2006 Turin Olympics, the Norwegian ski coach Bjornar Hakensmoen gave Canadian skier Sara Renner a ski pole after hers broke, and she and partner Beckie Scott went on to win silver in the team sprint. In gratitude, Canadians sent 7400 cans of maple syrup to Norway, where it is not a common treat.

Ruth's Unbaked Strawberry Cheesecake

Serves 8

Strawberries are usually ready for harvest by the end of June in many parts of Ontario, and the province is full of U-pick farms that feature this juicy berry. The name "strawberry" is derived from the Old English *streawberige*, with *streaw* meaning "straw" and *berige* meaning "berry." In parts of northern Europe, wild berries are still commonly gathered by threading them onto a straw, giving a possible origin for the name. Historically, strawberries (*Fragaria* species) were probably not widely eaten in Europe—although they were used occasionally for medicine, and the plants did become popular with the French nobility for their flowers. By the 1400s, however, strawberries were being sold on the streets of London. A large Chilean species of strawberry was first imported to Europe in 1714 and may have been the precursor to the large strawberries to which we have grown accustomed. Strawberries are a good source of vitamin C, so get them when they're fresh.

Crust
2 cups (500 mL) graham wafer crumbs

½ cup (125 mL) + 1 Tbsp (30 mL) unsalted butter, melted

zest of 1 lemon, finely chopped

Filling
3 x 250 g (8 oz) packages cream cheese, at room temperature

½ to 1 cup (125 to 250 mL) icing sugar, sifted

fresh lemon juice

⅓ cup (75 mL) whipping cream (32%)

Topping
1 x 8 oz (250 mL) jar of apple jelly

1 lb (500 g) strawberries, whole, washed and stemmed

Preheat oven to 350° F (175° C). Crush graham wafers with a rolling pin or pulse in a food processor to make crumbs. In a mixing bowl, combine the graham wafer crumbs, melted butter and lemon zest. Pat the mixture evenly into a 10-inch (25 cm) pie plate. Bake in the oven 10 minutes. Cool to room temperature. Cover and chill in the refrigerator until ready to fill. Crust can be made a day in advance.

In a food processor, combine cream cheese, icing sugar and a generous squeeze of lemon juice. Mix until smooth and creamy. Transfer into a large mixing bowl.

In a small bowl, beat the whipping cream until light and fluffy, and fold into the cream cheese mixture. Gently fill the chilled graham crust with the creamy filling and chill for at least 3 hours before serving.

To prepare the topping, gently heat the apple jelly until just warm in a small saucepan. In a medium bowl, pour the warm jelly over the strawberries and mix lightly. Arrange the glazed strawberries on top of the cheesecake.

Tip
You can use the bottom of a small glass to help press the graham wafer crumbs evenly on the pie plate.

Locally grown strawberries are tastier and jucier than the big ones imported from California.

Rhubarb Pie with a Meringue Crust

Serves 6

The English brought the first rhubarb to Canada. For early pioneers, these robust and hardy plants supplied essential vitamins and minerals in spring before any berries ripened. Patches of rhubarb can still be found dotting the Ontario landscape where no trace of a farmhouse remains. Indigenous to Asia, rhubarb (*Rheum* spp.) was first brought to Europe for its medicinal qualities. Marco Polo had a keen interest in it, and plantings were recorded in Italy as early as 1608. Huge plantations were soon established mainly for medicinal purposes in Oxfordshire and Bedfordshire, England, where they still grow today. Officially recognized in Europe as a food by the 17th century, rhubarb was for a time known as "pie plant," because it was most often presented as a pie filling and in other desserts.

1 cup (250 mL) sugar

3 Tbsp (45 mL) flour

1 tsp (5 mL) cinnamon

2 lbs (1 kg) rhubarb, frozen or fresh

1 x 9-inch (23 cm) pie crust, prebaked (or see p. 77 for Great Pie Crust)

Meringue

⅓ cup (60 mL) sugar

1 Tbsp (15 mL) cornstarch

5 egg whites

½ tsp (2 mL) cream of tartar

Mix together sugar, flour and cinnamon in a large bowl. Slice rhubarb into 1-inch (2.5 cm) pieces, add to the flour-sugar mixture and mix until well coated.

In a saucepan over medium heat, cook rhubarb until it is soft and thickened, about 10 minutes. Let cool for at least 30 minutes.

For the meringue, mix sugar and cornstarch in a small bowl. In another bowl, with an electric mixer, beat egg whites until foamy. Add cream of tartar and beat in sugar-cornstarch mixture, 1 Tbsp (15 mL) at a time, until egg whites are stiff and glossy.

Pour the cooled rhubarb filling into prepared pie crust and spoon meringue gently on top.

Bake the meringue-topped pie at 350° F (175° C) for 10 to 12 minutes, until the meringue is slightly golden.

A member of the buckwheat family, rhubarb is closely related to sorrel. Although rhubarb is technically a vegetable, the stems are used as a fruit in most recipes. Don't eat the leaves—they're poisonous.

Dandelion Wine

Makes about 12 bottles

Dandelion comes from the French, *dent de lion*, meaning lion's tooth. Spring marks the start of dandelion season and it's hard to believe they aren't native to Ontario. They were brought from Europe as an important vegetable plant, but they are now the bane of gardeners everywhere. The leaves are high in a variety of important vitamins, and the flowers are an important nectar source for insects such as bees in spring. You can also make a delicious wine using the blooms, as long as they haven't been treated with pesticides or herbicides. Ontario is the major wine-growing area of Canada, with wineries producing very fine wines for domestic and international markets. It seems fitting, then, to make wine out of this "weed" and perhaps improve the dandelion's image in the process.

about 15 cups (3.8 L) water

about 15 cups (3.8 L) dandelion blooms, washed and spun dry

juice of 3 lemons

3 oranges, peeled and sliced

2 cups (500 mL) unsulphured dried apricots

3 lbs (1.5 kg) granulated sugar

1 cake of brewer's yeast, available from your local home brewing store

Bring water to a boil and pour over the dandelion blooms in a large, clean, sterilized container that resists acids. Let sit for 24 hours.

Strain liquid and stir in lemon juice along with oranges, apricots, sugar and yeast. Let sit for 3 to 6 weeks, then strain again and bottle.

Age bottles at least 2 months before drinking.

Labrador Tea

The Labrador tea plant *(Ledum groenlandicum)* is related to blueberries and cranberries. The leaves have been used for centuries by the Native peoples in a tea, which is also known as swamp tea or Hudson Bay tea. Believed to possess medicinal qualities, it was applied topically for skin irritations and rashes and made into syrup for coughs and sour throats. It was also thought to aid in digestion and stimulate the nerves. Labrador tea is high in vitamin C, which was an important addition to the diet of the Natives and settlers alike.

To make Labrador tea, steep about 15 leaves in 4 cups (1 L) of boiling water for 8 minutes. Strain and serve, sweetened if desired.

Shaved Fennel Salad

Serves 4

Fennel has become naturalized along roadsides in southern Canada and grows well in Ontario, generally peaking in August. Native to southern Europe and parts of Asia, fennel *(Foeniculum vulgare)* is a tender, aromatic perennial herb with a distinct licorice flavour. Fennel is related to dill and, like its cousin, its seeds, leaves and flowers can all be enjoyed in everything from soups and salads to desserts. A variety of fennel called Florence fennel *(F. vulgare* var. *azoricum)* grows a swollen stem base that is used as a vegetable, either raw or cooked. Fennel is best eaten fresh, but the leaves can be frozen for later use in cooked dishes when fennel is out of season.

2 fennel bulbs, shaved paper thin, some fronds reserved for garnish

2 Tbsp (30 mL) extra virgin olive oil

1 Tbsp (15 mL) fresh lemon juice

1 tsp (5 mL) fresh thyme, chopped

¼ cup (60 mL) flat-leafed parsley, chopped

½ cup (125 mL) green olives, sliced

2 oranges, peeled and segmented

1 small red onion, sliced thin

sea salt and freshly ground pepper to taste

In a large bowl, mix all ingredients together and season with salt and pepper. Place on 4 plates, garnish with reserved fronds and serve.

Tip
Use a mandoline or meat slicer to shave the fennel bulbs.

Fennel is often mislabeled as anise, a related plant that bears seeds with a sharper licorice flavour that is perhaps best known for its starring role in absinthe.

Apple and Quinoa Salad

Serves 6 as a main-course salad

Quinoa is available in the grain section of large grocery stores, Bulk Barns and health food stores across Ontario. Known as the Mother Grain by the Incas, quinoa is not a grain at all, but a seed from a plant in the same family as spinach and buckwheat. Native to South America, it has a number of unusual qualities. Each seed is covered with saponin, a bitter natural residue that turns soapy in water and acts as a natural pesticide. Quinoa is higher in protein than any other grain; the United Nations has even classified it as a supercrop because it is such a complete foodstuff. The leaves of the quinoa plant are also edible and are used as a salad green.

juice from 1 lemon

⅓ cup (75 mL) apple cider vinegar

½ cup (125 mL) orange juice

⅓ cup (75 mL) canola or sunflower oil

⅓ cup (75 mL) honey

5 cups (1 L) cooked quinoa (see tip)

2 apples, cored and chopped

1 bell pepper, diced small

1 cup (250 mL) fresh corn kernels

½ cup (125 mL) dried cranberries

½ cup (125 mL) currants

1 small red onion, finely chopped

1 cup (250 mL) toasted, chopped pecans

1 cup (250 mL) fresh parsley and mint, chopped

sea salt and freshly ground pepper to taste

Place lemon juice, apple cider vinegar, orange juice, oil and honey in a small bowl and stir to combine. In a large bowl, combine quinoa and all remaining ingredients well, then stir in dressing. Adjust seasonings and refrigerate until ready to serve.

Tip

To cook quinoa, bring 4 cups (1 L) water to a boil in a wide-bottomed pot with a lid. Add a pinch of salt and stir in 2 cups (500 mL) quinoa. Reduce heat to a simmer, cover and cook until all the water is absorbed, about 25 minutes. You can cook any amount of quinoa you like as long as you keep the 2:1 ratio of liquid to grain. It is also worth experimenting with other liquids such as stock or coconut milk.

Tip

If there is any leftover quinoa, you can warm it up and add a little cinnamon and cream for a nice breakfast.

Tomato Salad with Bocconcini Tempura

Serves 4

If you're vacationing near Ottawa, be sure to try some locally grown tomatoes. The mineral content of the soil in eastern Ontario produces some of the best-tasting tomatoes in Ontario. Heirloom tomatoes have become more popular recently simply because of their incredible flavour. Over the years, heirloom varieties have been lost or replaced by hybrid tomatoes, which have been bred more for their commercial value than for their taste. There's nothing like eating a fresh, garden heirloom tomato, so check for them at farmers' markets or try growing them yourself from seed—the taste is worth the extra effort.

peanut oil

1 lb (500 g) assorted heirloom tomatoes, sliced into thick rounds

handful of fresh basil

17 oz (500 ml) container mini bocconcini, drained and patted very dry

1 recipe of tempura batter (see p. 146)

extra virgin olive oil or cold-pressed canola oil

juice of 1 lemon

sea salt and freshly ground pepper

Heat peanut oil in pot or deep fryer to 375° F (190° C). Arrange sliced tomato and basil onto individual plates. Dip bocconcini into tempura batter and fry until golden. Serve tempura bocconcini together with tomato slices, drizzle with canola oil and lemon juice. Season with salt and pepper.

Tip
For deep-frying, peanut oil should be 2 to 3 inches (5 to 7.5 cm) deep in pot or use deep fryer according to the manufacturer's directions.

Honey-drizzled Figs with Pecan-crusted Goat Cheese

Serves 6

Be sure to seek out and treat yourself to some of these delicious fruits when they come into season. Fresh figs are available mostly in the fall. Delicate, with a heady sweetness, fresh figs are ripe when they yield to soft pressure. They have a short shelf life and should be enjoyed within a few days of purchase. If your usual grocer doesn't have them, try Italian or other Mediterranean markets.

1 x 8 oz (250 g) goat cheese log (chèvre)

1 cup (250 mL) toasted, chopped pecans, plus halves for garnish

1 lb (500 g) baby mixed lettuce

⅓ cup (75 mL) extra virgin olive oil

sea salt and freshly ground pepper

12 fresh figs, any variety

½ cup (125 mL) fireweed honey

Roll goat cheese log in nuts, and wrap in cellophane. Refrigerate at least ½ hour and up to 6 hours.

Arrange lettuce onto 6 plates and sprinkle lightly with olive oil. Season with salt and pepper. Cut figs into halves and arrange atop greens.

Slice cheese into 6 equal-sized rounds and place next to figs. Drizzle with honey, season lightly again with salt and pepper and serve.

Figs are probably the oldest cultivated crop. In June 2006 archaeological evidence near the ancient city of Jericho placed fig remains at 11,400 years old. Fig trees are mentioned in the Bible.

Wild Salmon en Papillote

Serves 4

Once abundant in the Great Lakes, the freshwater Atlantic salmon became extinct by the late 1890s owing to mill dams, overfishing and habitat destruction. In an attempt to restock the lakes with salmon, Pacific salmon varieties, namely chinook (*Oncorhynchus tshawytsch*) and coho (*O. kisutch*), were introduced. Today, chinook and coho salmon are found in all of the Great Lakes of the province, with annual chinook stocking levels in excess of 1.6 million. There are two main types of salmon fishing in Ontario. Charter boats are a popular way to head out on the lake with a guide, who will help you reel in a big one, or, in the late summer when the salmon move inshore, you can fish for salmon right from the shore of Ashbridge's Bay, within sight of downtown Toronto.

4 wild salmon fillets, 4 to 6 oz (125 to 170 g) each

4 leeks, white parts only, sliced thin and well washed

¼ cup (60 mL) dry white wine

sea salt and freshly ground pepper

1 bunch dill or other fresh herb, chopped

¼ cup (60 mL) unsalted butter, cut into 4 pieces

1 egg white, lightly beaten

1 lemon, sliced

Heat oven to 350° F (175° C). Fold a 24-inch (60 cm) sheet of parchment paper in half, and cut out a heart shape about 4 inches (10 cm) larger than a fish fillet. Place fillet near the fold, and place a handful of leeks next to it, sprinkle with wine, salt, pepper and dill and top with a piece of butter. Brush edges of parchment paper with the egg white, fold paper to enclose fish, and make small overlapping folds to seal the edges, starting at curve of heart. Be sure each fold overlaps the one before it to create an airtight seal. Repeat with rest of fillets. Put packages on a baking sheet, and bake until paper is puffed and brown, about 10 to 15 minutes. Serve salmon in the packets with lemon slices and sautéed vegetables. Be careful of steam when opening the packets.

Cooking in parchment paper, *en papillote in French, is an easy, low-fat way to pre-pare fish. The word* papillote *is derived from* papillon, *meaning butterfly, and hence, why the parchment pouch is traditionally folded into a heart or butterfly shape. Try cooking vegetables in parchment as well.*

Blackened Walleye with Oven-dried Tomatoes

Serves 2

With over 400,000 lakes, rivers and streams, Ontario is an angler's paradise. The favourite Ontario freshwater fish is the walleye (*Sander vitreus vitreus*), a tasty fish with golden flesh and eyes that reflect light for those evening fishing excursions. You can start fishing for walleye in the late spring throughout the province. Other popular Ontario fish include pike, bass, trout and muskie. All of these wild fish taste great, but they're also are great fun to catch—or catch and release.

2 lbs (1 kg) Roma tomatoes, halved lengthwise

3 cloves garlic, minced

¼ cup (60 mL) fresh thyme, chopped

sea salt and freshly ground black pepper to taste

½ cup (125 mL) extra virgin olive oil

Spice Mixture

2 tsp (10 mL) paprika

2 tsp (10 mL) chipotle powder or chili powder

2 tsp (10 mL) ground cumin

2 tsp (10 mL) dried thyme

1 tsp (5 mL) freshly ground black pepper

1 tsp (5 mL) sea salt

2 fresh walleye, gutted but whole

2 Tbsp (30 mL) canola oil

Preheat the oven to 250 F (120° C).

Scoop out seeds from the tomatoes. Mix the garlic with the thyme, salt and pepper and olive oil. Place the tomatoes cut side up in a roasting pan and drizzle with the garlic mixture. Bake for at least 3 hours or until the tomatoes are dehydrated but still chewy.

Mix all the spices together in a bowl.

Rinse walleye with water and pat dry with paper towels. Brush oil on the walleye and rub the spice mixture all over.

Heat a heavy-bottomed skillet until it is smoking hot. Place the prepared walleye in the skillet and cook for 2 to 4 minutes and turn over. Cook until the walleye is firm and cooked through, 3 to 4 minutes. To test doneness, the fish should flake easily with a fork but should not be dry. Serve with oven-dried tomatoes on the side.

Tip

Oven-drying tomatoes is a great way to preserve these tasty bits of summer sunshine. Grow tomatoes in your garden or in containers, or pick them up at farmers' markets.

Tip

Any leftover tomatoes can be covered in olive oil and stored in a jar. They will keep for up to 3 weeks refrigerated.

Grilled Beef Tenderloin with Sautéed Chanterelles

Serves 4

Kerr Farms of Chatham, Ontario, raises "back to nature" grass-fed beef that they claim is a healthier option than grain-fed beef. Their Angus cattle graze on a natural diet of grasses and legumes, so the meat is less fatty and contains more Omega 3 essential fatty acids—the result is a tastier, more nutritious beef. In this recipe, succulent tenderloin is paired with wild chanterelles. Chanterelles, which range from pale yellow to yellow-brown, grow wild in moist, woodland habitats throughout Ontario. Efforts to cultivate chanterelles commercially in the province have so far been unsuccessful.

4 beef tenderloin medallions, about 6 to 8 oz (170 to 250 g) each

olive oil, for brushing

2 tsp (10 mL) kosher salt

freshly ground black pepper

Mushrooms

1 to 2 Tbsp (15 to 30 mL) olive oil

3 shallots, sliced

1 lb (500 g) fresh chanterelles

1 clove garlic, minced

½ cup (125 mL) white wine

1 cup (250 mL) parsley, chopped

¼ cup (60 mL) chives, chopped

sea salt and freshly ground black pepper

Remove beef medallions from refrigerator 15 minutes before cooking.

To prepare the mushrooms, heat olive oil in a skillet over medium-high heat and sauté the shallots until soft. Add chanterelles, garlic and continue to sauté for 5 to 7 minutes, then add white wine and cook until the liquid evaporates. Remove from heat and stir in parsley and chives. Season with salt and pepper.

Prepare a grill or a stove-top grill pan with a medium-high heat fire. Brush beef lightly with olive oil and season with salt and pepper and place on the grill and cook, without moving it, until nice grill marks appear, about 4 minutes. Turn the medallions and continue to grill until an instant-read thermometer inserted into the medallions sideways registers about 120° F (50° C), about 3 to 4 minutes more. Set aside on a cutting board to rest for 5 minutes before serving.

Divide medallions among plates and spoon on the mushrooms.

Mu Shu Duck with Peaches and Daikon

Serves 4

Game birds were an important food source for Canada's indigenous peoples, and early settlers soon learned to hunt them as well. Geese, wild turkey, partridge, quail and, of course, duck have always been abundant in Ontario, at least seasonally, offering both a nutritious food source and sport for hunters. Probably the best-known species of duck, the mallard *(Anas platyrhynchos),* is also Ontario's most common duck. Mariposa Farm, a family-run farm located 45 minutes out of Ottawa, offers a variety of duck and geese products, from fresh meat to pâtés and mousses, from the farm gate. The Walker-Lavoie family also hosts private functions for up to 50 people in a rustic country setting.

Duck

8 oz (250 g) duck breast, about 2 breasts, cut into strips

3 Tbsp (45 mL) rice vinegar

2 Tbsp (30 mL) soy sauce

1 tsp (5 mL) sesame oil

1 Tbsp (15 mL) garlic, minced

1 Tbsp (15 mL) fresh ginger, finely chopped

grape seed or canola oil for stir frying

½ cup (125 mL) green onions, finely sliced

Daikon

1 daikon radish, 4-inch (10 cm) piece, grated

1 Tbsp (15 mL) rice vinegar

½ tsp (2 mL) sugar

1 Tbsp (15 mL) green onion, finely sliced

In a bowl, toss the duck with the rice vinegar, soy sauce, sesame oil, garlic and ginger. Cover and marinate, refrigerated, for 2 hours. In another bowl, toss the daikon with rice vinegar, sugar and green onion. Set aside.

Heat a splash of grape seed oil in a wok (or heavy-bottomed pan) and add the marinated duck strips. Stir fry over high heat until

browned and cooked through, about 3 minutes. Remove from the pan, toss with green onions and set aside. Reduce the heat to medium and cook peaches in the wok for 5 minutes, set aside. Add a splash of oil to the wok and cook eggs, sunny side up.

Serve duck, daikon, peaches, eggs, enoki mushrooms on a platter along with side serving plates. Spread a spoonful of hoisin sauce on a flatbread and place some meat, peaches and vegetables on top, roll up and enjoy.

2 fresh peaches, cut into eighths

4 large eggs

4 oz (125 g) fresh enoki mushrooms

hoisin sauce

1 package store-bought flatbread, such as chapati

Hemp Heart and Lentil Burgers

Serves 4

Ontario is Canada's third largest producer of hemp—it is also the home to North America's first bred and registered variety of hemp, "Anka." Hemp (*Cannabis sativa*) is an annual herb that has been grown since the Stone Age for its fibre, which up until the 14th century was more common than linen. Hemp has been used to make paper, clothing and rope, and like flax, is also an important food source. Hemp seeds and oil are the two most popular forms of hemp as a food, which is high in quality essential fatty acids and second only to raw, uncooked soybeans as a source of protein. Canada has allowed the industrialized production of hemp since 1998, putting this country in the ranks of other forward-thinking nations that recognize the potential benefits this versatile crop has to offer.

1 x 19 oz (540 ml) can lentils

½ cup (125 mL) hemp hearts

1 small carrot, grated

1 egg

1 Tbsp (15 mL) ketchup

⅓ cup (75 mL) dry bread crumbs

1 small onion, finely chopped

1 clove garlic, minced

1 Tbsp (15 mL) thyme, chopped

salt and freshly ground pepper to taste

dash hot pepper sauce (optional)

1 to 2 Tbsp (15 to 30 mL) canola or sunflower oil

Place lentils, hemp hearts and carrot in a medium bowl and mix well (your hands work best for this). Stir in egg, ketchup, bread crumbs, onion, garlic and thyme, salt and pepper and if using, hot pepper sauce. Cover and refrigerate for 1 hour.

Shape lentil mixture into four ½-inch-thick (1 cm) patties. Heat oil in a skillet over medium heat and cook patties until browned on each side. Alternatively, brush patties with oil and grill until browned, about 5 minutes for each side. Serve on buns with your favourite condiments.

Ingersoll is home to North America's first one-acre hemp maze!

Hemp hearts are shelled hemp seeds, which have a subtle nutty flavour similar to flax seeds. They are available at health food stores, grocery stores and on the Internet.

Eggplant Lasagna

Serves 6 to 8

Like tomatoes, peppers and potatoes, eggplants (*Solanum melongena*) come in a wide variety of shapes and colours, although globe-shaped varieties such as "Black Beauty" are most common. Eggplants need a lot of sun and heat to grow, so most Ontario farms grow their eggplants in a hothouse to secure a reliable supply. Like the related tomato, eggplant got off to a slow start in European gardens outside of the Mediterranean, except as an ornamental plant. Eggplant is unique in the nightshade family as the only member to have originated in Asia, specifically in India and China. By the way, eggplant gets its name because early varieties introduced to Europe were white and looked like eggs! In some countries, eggplant is known as aubergine.

1 large eggplant, sliced ½ inch (1 cm) thick, crosswise

1 medium zucchini, sliced ½ inch (1 cm) thick

2 to 3 Tbsp (30 to 45 mL) olive oil

2 Tbsp (30 mL) butter

Tomato Sauce

1 Tbsp (15 mL) olive oil

2 large onions, finely chopped

3 or 4 cloves garlic, minced

2 bay leaves

splash of red wine

2 cups (500 mL) canned plum tomatoes, roughly chopped

12 sheets oven-ready lasagna noodles

2 cups (500 mL) freshly grated Asiago cheese

sea salt and freshly ground pepper to taste

Toss eggplant and zucchini slices with olive oil and season with salt and pepper. Grill on a stovetop grill or barbecue for 5 minutes on each side. Set aside.

Preheat oven to 375° F (190° C). Warm oil and butter in a heavy-based casserole over medium heat. Add onion and sauté for about 5 minutes until softened and translucent. Add garlic and cook for another couple of minutes, stirring to coat well. Cook gently for about 5 minutes. Season with nutmeg, salt and pepper. Pour in wine and simmer until it has evaporated, then add tomatoes with their juice and stir thoroughly. Cook, uncovered, for 30 minutes. Taste and correct seasoning.

For ricotta mixture, combine ingredients in medium bowl. Season to taste and set aside.

For béchamel, pour milk into a saucepan with bay leaf, onion and a generous pinch of nutmeg. Bring to just below the boiling point, then remove from heat and leave to infuse for 10 minutes. Strain the milk to remove the bay leaf and onion.

Melt butter in a saucepan and stir in the flour. Cook, stirring, for 5 minutes. Pour the hot milk into the flour mixture. Cook on low heat, stirring frequently, for 10 minutes until thickened. Season the sauce with salt and pepper and set aside.

To assemble, start by buttering a 13 x 9 x 3-inch (33 x 23 x 5 cm) baking pan. Pour some béchamel into the baking pan—enough to just cover the bottom. Top with a layer of lasagna, add béchamel, a layer of grilled vegetables, tomato sauce, then more béchamel and a good handful of Asiago cheese. Cover with lasagna, then the ricotta mixture. Top with lasagna, then béchamel, vegetables, tomato sauce. Add another layer of lasagna and top with béchamel. Add a final sprinkling of Asiago cheese. Bake in oven for 30 to 40 minutes, until browned and bubbling all over.

Tip

Older eggplants will have an acrid flavour, so choose freshly picked, if possible. Alternatively, you can remove most of the bitter flavour by salting the sliced eggplant and letting it sit for 10 to 15 minutes. Gently squeeze out the bitter liquid, rinse lightly in cold water and pat dry on a paper towel.

Tip

You can add as many layers as you wish, depending on the depth of your pan.

Ricotta Mixture

2 cups (500 g) ricotta cheese

½ cup (125 mL) freshly grated Parmesan cheese

½ cup (125 mL) freshly grated Mozzarella cheese

sea salt and freshly ground pepper

Béchamel

3 cups (750 mL) milk

2 bay leaves

1 onion, halved

pinch of freshly grated nutmeg

¼ cup (60 mL) butter

¼ cup (60 mL) flour

sea salt and freshly ground pepper

Summer Squash Ratatouille

Serves 4 as a main course, 6 as a side dish

The only difference between summer squash and winter squash is when we eat them. All squash mature in a similar fashion, developing hard rinds and storing for months. Summer squash are best eaten before they mature and develop any bitter flavour, while winter squash retain their flavour and texture once they have ripened. You can grow both types in your garden and can eat either kind when they are immature or mature. Most squash are ready in about 50 to 90 days from sowing to harvest. Early Native peoples in North and South America discovered that members of the squash family (*Cucurbitaceae*) love to cross-pollinate, giving them an abundant and interesting mix of plants to choose from.

1 medium eggplant, 2½ lbs (1.2 kg),
cut into ½ in (1 cm) cubes

olive oil for cooking

1 lb (500 g) assorted summer squash,
as much variety as possible,
cut into ½ in (1 cm) slices

2 medium onions, sliced

2 red bell peppers, seeded and
cut into ½ in (1 cm) strips

3 ripe but firm tomatoes about 1 lb (500 g),
seeded and quartered

2 cloves garlic, minced

⅓ cup (75 mL) of a mixture of chopped fresh
rosemary, thyme, basil, fennel and marjoram

pinch of dried lavender

sea salt and freshly ground
black pepper to taste

French bread

Lay the eggplant cubes on paper towels and sprinkle with salt. Let them sit for 15 minutes, then rinse and pat dry.

Have a large bowl ready. Heat a splash of olive oil in a large skillet or casserole over medium heat. Add the eggplant chunks and cook until they start to soften, remove from pan and set aside in the bowl to make room for the next vegetable. Add more olive oil, as needed, and continue with the squash, onions and peppers separately.
Return all vegetables to pan; add tomatoes, garlic and herbs. Season with salt

and pepper and stir to mix. Simmer over medium heat until much of the liquid is evaporated, about 10 minutes, then cover, turn heat to medium low and cook until the vegetables are tender, about 45 minutes to 1 hour, stirring occasionally to prevent sticking. Serve at room temperature with crusty French bread.

Tip

Squash blossoms are also edible and make a great vessel for stuffing and deep frying. Make sure you choose the male stems (but leave a few for pollination) and leave the fruit-bearing females for an abundant summer supply.

Ratatouille is a vegetable dish from the Provençal region of southern France. Its main ingredients are tomatoes, eggplant and zucchini, although there are countless variations, including this one. It's also good cold if you have leftovers.

Char-grilled Corn with Jalapeño Lime Butter

Corn is Canada's third largest crop and seventy percent of Canada's corn is grown in Ontario. The importance of corn as a crop could also take on a huge environmental role, as items traditionally made from petroleum, such as plastic packaging, are now being made from biodegradable cornhusks. Corn (Zea mays) is native to the Americas, and its history dates back thousands of years. The first corn was probably a popcorn variety, and it wasn't until its introduction to European settlers that sweet corn strains started to emerge. Sadly, in the quest for sweet corn, we have lost many of the hundreds of varieties that were once common.

ears of corn

jalapeño lime butter (see below)

lime wedges

sea salt to taste

Jalapeño Lime Butter

1 cup (250 mL) unsalted butter, softened

1 jalapeño pepper, seeded and finely chopped

zest from 1 lime

1 clove garlic, minced

1 tsp (5 mL) sea salt

Preheat the barbecue to medium-high heat. Peel back the husks, leaving them attached, and remove the silk from the corn. Rewrap, tying with butcher twine or kitchen string if necessary. Barbecue for about 10 minutes, turning to cook all sides. If husks start to burn, spritz with water.

Serve hot corn with rounds of the jalapeño lime butter, lime wedges and sea salt.

Jalapeño Lime Butter
Mix the ingredients together in a bowl or in a food processor. Wrap in plastic and shape into a cylinder about an inch (2.5 cm) in diameter, and refrigerate.

Corn is really a grain, though we generally eat it fresh, as a vegetable.

Tip
To keep the sugars from turning to starch, keep freshly picked corn as cool as possible and enjoy it soon after harvesting. Fresh corn can be steamed, boiled or grilled, and older corn can be cut from the cob and added to soups and stews.

Barbecued Ontario Peaches with Camembert

Serves 6

Peaches (*Prunus persica*) come into season in Ontario in mid-July. After British Columbia, southern Ontario is Canada's most important peach-growing area, and peaches have flourished here since the time of the first European settlers. The Niagara fruit belt produces 90 percent of Ontario's peaches. If you really want to experience the essence of Ontario's peaches, be sure to head out to the Winona Peach Festival, which is held every year from August 25 to 27. Nectarines, though thought of as a different fruit, are actually a variety of peach with a smooth skin, and it is not uncommon for a peach tree to produce a few nectarines and vice versa.

6 peaches, pitted and sliced in half

2 Tbsp (30 mL) canola or grape seed oil

1 Tbsp (15 mL) honey

pinch of sea salt

pinch of pepper

4 oz (125 g) Camembert, cut into wedges

6 fresh basil leaves

Preheat barbecue to medium-high. Combine oil, honey, salt and pepper in a bowl. Brush peaches with glaze and grill flesh side down for 3 minutes. Place peaches flesh side up on a baking sheet and place a basil leaf and a wedge of Camembert on top of each peach. Return the peaches on baking sheet to the barbecue, close the lid and cook until the cheese is melted, about 5 minutes.

Peaches are the stone fruit from a tree that originated in China, where peaches are an important symbol for a long life and immortality.

Onions are extremely versatile to have on hand. You can use them raw, sautéed, caramelized and deep-fried, and there are many types of onions available in Ontario. Red onions are usually used in Greek salads, and white and yellow onions are ubiquitous. This is a recipe for savoury jam, suitable for serving with meats such as roast beef. I paired it here with a cheese and crackers tray as part of an after-dinner treat, but it works equally well as an appetizer.

¼ cup (60 mL) olive oil

6 medium sweet onions, sliced thinly

pinch sea salt

1 Tbsp (15 mL) balsamic vinegar

¼ cup (60 mL) port

sprig of fresh thyme

½ cup (120 mL) muscovado sugar

1 tsp (5 mL) mustard seeds

½ tsp (2 mL) red pepper flakes

¼ cup (60 mL) tomato, finely chopped

Melt the oil in heavy frying pan. Add the onions and sauté until slightly brown. Season with salt. Reduce the heat, then continue to cook, stirring constantly, until caramelized and tender. Add the remaining ingredients, except the tomato, and cook on low heat for 30 minutes, stirring occasionally. Add the tomato and cook for 15 more minutes. Let cool and store in a jar in the refrigerator. Keeps for 2 weeks refrigerated.

Try onion jam on pizzas and sandwiches.

Iced Tea with Fresh Mint

Serves 4

Across Ontario, no fewer than 150 tearooms serve a variety of teas, both iced and hot. You can even sign your children up for tea and etiquette parties at historic sites such as Fulford Place, overlooking the St. Lawrence River. Tea is gaining popularity as we strive towards a healthier lifestyle, and sipping afternoon tea at the local teahouse is becoming a favourite pastime. Traditionally, iced tea was served as a refreshing punch spiked with alcohol. The version we think of most often today, the one that is freshly brewed tea sweetened and flavoured with lemon, first became popular after being served at the 1904 St. Louis World's Fair. Iced tea can be made with any tea you like, from the standard black tea to green tea, and even caffeine-free herbal tea.

6 cups (1.5 L) cold water

5 level tsp (25 mL) good quality, loose tea

⅔ cup (150 mL) white sugar, or to taste

handful of fresh mint, rinsed and patted dry

1 lime or lemon

Bring water to a boil. Place the tea in a pitcher and pour the boiling water over the tea. Let infuse for 30 minutes.

Stir in sugar to dissolve and strain tea into a clean pitcher. Add the remaining water.

Bruise the mint by crushing it lightly with a rolling pin or the bottom of a glass and place in the pitcher.

Chill tea for at least 1 hour. Remove mint and serve with a wedge of lime or lemon and a sprig of mint, if desired.

Some people call the alcohol-spiked version of iced tea "iced tea on a stick." Iced coffee is also a popular summer drink available homemade or purchased from fine coffee shops throughout the province.

Yogurt and Honey Semifreddo

Serves 4 to 6

In the early 17th century, Europeans introduced honeybees into North America. The bees soon escaped from the domestic hives, established wild colonies and began to flourish. Today, there are well over half a million bee colonies in Canada, with over 75,000 of those in Ontario. The bees' efforts not only provide honey but also offer an invaluable pollination service to farmers. In fact, the value of bees to agriculture is worth 10 to 20 times the value of all honey and bee products combined. Bees are crucial to cranberry production, for example, and are "employed" during the spring to pollinate the crops. Honey is sweeter than table sugar, and its flavour varies depending on the type of flowers visited by the bees that produced it. The average Canadian eats over 4.5 pounds (2 kg) of honey per year.

2¼ cups (560 mL) heavy cream (32%)

5 egg yolks

½ cup (125 mL) honey

½ cup (125 mL) unflavoured yogurt

In a mixer, whisk cream to stiff peaks. Transfer the whipped cream into another bowl and set aside. Clean and dry the mixing bowl and whisk yolks with honey until pale yellow and thickened. Fold in yogurt. Then fold in whipped cream.

Line a mould with plastic wrap. Place filling into the mold. Cover and freeze for 24 hours. Remove semifreddo from the freezer just before serving. Top with your favourite berries.

Semifreddo is Italian for "half-cold" and describes the half-frozen or chilled nature of this delicious confection.

Cherry Pie

Serves 6 to 8

A member of the same family of fruits as peaches and almonds, cherries are available in Ontario from June through early August. There are two types of cherry, the sweet cherry and the sour cherry. Hedelfingen cherries are Ontario's most popular sweet cherry because they resist cracking under our humid conditions. The Montmorency is a sour variety and the most commonly grown cherry in Ontario. It is used for cooking, baking and jams. Of all the varieties of cherries, the Montmorency has the highest level of anthocyanins, natural pain and inflammation inhibitors. First Nations peoples knew the benefits of cherries and used wild varieties to treat inflammation, fever and sore throats.

6 cups (1.5 L) fresh pitted cherries

¾ cup (175 mL) sugar

juice from a lemon

2 Tbsp (30 mL) cornstarch

pastry (see opposite)

Preheat oven to 400° F (200° C). In a medium saucepan, mix cherries and sugar and cook over medium-low heat until most of the juice from the cherries has reduced, about 15 minutes. Stir the lemon juice and cornstarch together in a small bowl and add to the cherries. Cook, stirring until thick, about 7 minutes. Remove from heat and let cool to room temperature.

Pour cherry filling into a prepared pastry crust and bake for 10 minutes. Reduce heat to 375° F (190° C) and bake for 20 to 30 minutes or until pastry is golden brown. Let it cool before serving.

Sunnybrook Farms of Niagara-on-the-Lake is renowned for making wine from fruits other than grapes. Their Montmorency cherry wine is one of their best.

Great Pie Crust

Mix flour, salt and sugar in a bowl. Using your cheese grater, grate frozen butter into flour mixture. Toss lightly to distribute butter and add lemon juice and enough water for dough just to come together. Divide in half, wrap each piece in plastic wrap and flatten into a disc. Chill for at least 30 minutes before using. Makes enough for a double-crusted pie.

2½ cups (625 mL) flour

1 tsp (5 mL) sea salt

1 Tbsp (15 mL) sugar

1 cup (250 mL) unsalted butter, frozen

1 Tbsp (15 mL) lemon juice

about ⅓ cup (75 mL) ice water

Tip

To make a lattice top, roll out and cut the remaining piece of dough into 1" (2.5 cm) strips. Interlock the strips in a criss-cross weave over the pie filling and press the strips onto the edges of the bottom crust. Brush the pastry lightly with a glaze made with 1 beaten egg and 2 Tbsp (30 mL) milk.

Currant Cooler

Serves 2

Currants are members of the genus *Ribes*, which includes the edible currants (black currant, red currant and white currant), gooseberries and many ornamental plants. They are native to the temperate regions of the Northern Hemisphere and grow well in Ontario. Black currants are the most popular variety grown here, with several hundred hectares dedicated to this berry. Black currants produce more juice per hectare than oranges and are also higher in vitamin C. Currants are at their peak in August and are available at many U-pick farms around the province. They also make beautiful fruit-bearing shrubs for any yard.

6 oz (180 mL) currant juice

4 oz (120 mL) frozen vodka

3 drops dry vermouth

frozen currants for garnish

2 martini glasses

ice

Fill shaker ½ full of ice. Pour in vodka, dry vermouth and currant juice. Shake and strain. Pour into martini glasses and garnish with frozen currants.

Black currants are native to Ontario, but didn't become a popular cultivated crop until several disease-resistant varieties were developed at the University of Guelph. They are now becoming more popular with gardeners and commercial growers alike.

Raspberry Tart

Serves 6 to 8

Fragrant, sweet and subtly tart, raspberries (*Rubus* spp.) are a favourite Ontario fruit. Members of the rose family, raspberries grown in Ontario are mostly of the ruby red variety, such as the "Boyne" or "Killarney," but purple, black and yellow varieties are becoming more popular. Raspberry production here peaks in July and lasts through to September. Raspberries are healthy, antioxidant-rich berries, high in ellagic acid—the same family of tannins that make wine, green tea and fruit such as pomegranates an important part of a healthier lifestyle. Raspberries are also an excellent source of manganese, vitamin C and dietary fibre, and the leaves make a soothing herbal tea.

Crust

1¼ cups (310 mL)
all-purpose flour

¼ cup (60 mL) sugar

½ cup (125 mL) or 1 stick
unsalted butter, cold and
cut into pieces

2 to 3 Tbsp (30 to 45 mL)
cold water

Filling

2 x 8 oz containers (275 g)
mascarpone,
room temperature

½ cup (125 mL) sugar

1 tsp (5 mL) vanilla

3 cups (750 mL) raspberries,
picked over

Glaze

1 x 8 oz (250 mL) jar of
apple jelly

For the crust, place flour, sugar and butter in a food processor and blend until mixture resembles coarse meal. Add 2 Tbsp (30 mL) of the water until incorporated. Add enough remaining water, if necessary, until mixture comes together but is still crumbly. Wrap dough in plastic and refrigerate for 1 hour.

Preheat oven to 350° F (175° C). Press crust mixture evenly onto bottom and sides of an 11-inch (28 cm) tart pan with removable fluted rim or 6 to 8 individual tart tins. Prick crust with a fork, line it with parchment and weigh it down with pie weights or dried beans. Bake in middle of oven until golden, about 15 minutes. Let cool to room temperature and chill for 1 hour in refrigerator.

Make the filling while the crust chills. In a bowl, using an electric mixer, beat mascarpone, sugar and vanilla together until smooth. Pour filling into chilled crust, spreading evenly, and arrange raspberries on top.

If keeping the tart longer than a day, brush raspberries lightly with a glaze of warmed apple jelly.

Tip
When out picking raspberries in your yard or favourite U-pick farm, be sure to keep them as cool as possible (ideally, pick them during cooler times of the day or on a cloudy day), and store them unwashed.

Mascarpone is a rich cream cheese that has the consistency of a stiff whipped cream. Originally produced in the Lombardy region of Italy, it is now available in grocery stores and Italian markets.

Blueberry Ice Cream

Makes 4 cups (1 L)

Blueberries, which grow across much of the country, were a significant food source for Canada's indigenous peoples, and parts of the plant were also important in medical uses. A favourite Inuit preparation of blueberries is to preserve them in fish oil. About half of Canada's commercial blueberry harvest comes from cultivated highbush varieties (*Vaccinium corymbosum*), with the rest supplied by managed stands of wild lowbush berries (*V. angustifolium* and *V. myrtilloides*). "Wild blues" are smaller, with a deeper blue colour and more intense blueberry flavour than the cultivated berries. Most of the blueberries grown in Ontario are of the highbush variety, producing a higher yield and a larger berry. Bursting with flavour, full of antioxidants and containing very few calories, blueberries are said to be among the healthiest of foods. Lowbush blueberries are common on the Canadian Shield and hikers often add them to their lunches.

1 cup (250 mL) whole milk (3%)

3 cups (750 mL) heavy cream (32%)

1 vanilla bean, split lengthwise

5 egg yolks

¾ cup (175 mL) sugar

2½ cups (625 mL) washed blueberries

In a heavy-bottomed saucepan, heat milk, cream and vanilla bean until just before boiling, stirring occasionally. Remove from heat, take out vanilla bean, scrape out the seeds and add them to the milk. Set aside.

In a mixing bowl, whisk the egg yolks and sugar until pale yellow and thickened. Slowly pour about 1 cup (250 mL) of the hot mixture into the egg yolks, whisking constantly. Add the yolk mixture back into the rest of the cream and cook over medium heat, stirring constantly, until the mixture thickens and coats the back of a spoon. Be sure not to let the mixture boil at any time or it will curdle. Pour through a fine strainer into a bowl, add blueberries and freeze in an ice cream maker according to the manufacturer's instructions.

Many people fondly remember the ice cream sold by vendors travelling the streets of their neighbourhoods during long, hot summer days of their childhood. Even today the familiar music wafting through open windows makes us all want to "scream for ice cream."

Yogurt with Flaxseed and Maple Syrup

Serves 1

Flax is a minor crop in Ontario, mostly grown in Bruce County and North Huron County. However, Canada is the largest producer and exporter of flax worldwide, most of it being grown in the endless fields of Saskatchewan. Louis Hébert, the first farmer in what is now Canada, brought flax (*Linum usitatissimum*) to New France in 1617. Flaxseeds are the most concentrated vegetable source of omega-3 fatty acid and are among the very best sources of both soluble and insoluble dietary fibre. Flaxseeds are used in many products and may be whole, ground or pressed into oil. They are used in baking and pet food; they are even a popular addition to the diet of laying hens to produce omega-3-enriched "designer eggs."

1 cup (250 mL) plain yogurt

ground golden flaxseed

pure maple syrup to taste

fresh fruit of your choice

This really isn't a recipe, but rather a list of ingredients that are tasty together as well as being healthy for you. Flaxseeds have a lovely nutty flavour, in addition to thickening the yogurt. I use 2 Tbsp (30 mL) of flaxseed, but you can add any amount you like.

Mix yogurt, flaxseed and maple syrup together and garnish with fruit.

Here's something I'll bet you didn't know: 1 Tbsp (15 mL) of ground flaxseeds and ¼ cup (60 ml) of water = 1 egg. Well, it replaces an egg in most baking, such as cakes and cookies, but the substitution doesn't work for foods such as meringues or omelettes.

Fruit Smoothie

Serves 1

Berries were an important part of the First Nations peoples' lives long before the first Europeans came to Canada. Berries were eaten fresh, dried or preserved in oil. They were used for dyes, medicine and even jewellery. Learning to use indigenous foods such as berries often sustained early settlers during their first months in Canada. Today, Ontario has over 200 registered berry growers, the majority of them growing strawberries and raspberries. Blueberries, currants, gooseberries and even the prairie jewel—saskatoons—are also grown in the province, many available in season at U-pick farms and farmers' markets.

**1 banana, peeled,
cut and frozen**

**¾ cup (175 mL) fresh or
frozen berries**

¼ cup (60 mL) coconut milk

1 cup (250 mL) vanilla soy milk

1 Tbsp (15 mL) almond butter

¼ cup (60 mL) crushed ice

Purée all ingredients in a blender until smooth.

Tip
Coconut milk from a can will keep in the fridge for 4 to 5 days.

Fruit smoothies are perfect for breakfast. Try experimenting with different fruits or fresh fruit juices.

Spiced Parsnip and Cauliflower Soup

Serves 4 to 6

With its elegant ivory colour and sweet, complex flavour, the parsnip (*Pastinaca sativa*) is the queen of root vegetables. It can be used in everything from soups and main courses to fragrant, crispy garnishes. A favourite throughout Europe, the parsnip has been cultivated there since medieval times. Parsnips came to Canada in the 17th century, and today over 100 hectares (247 acres) of Ontario farmland is dedicated to its production. This root crop is a member of the parsley family, which also includes carrots and celery. It is especially well suited to a short growing season in a cooler climate. Parsnips are best enjoyed in late autumn, once they have benefited from exposure to frost. Unlike its cousin the carrot, the parsnip has no vitamin A, but it does boast a higher vitamin C content.

2 to 3 Tbsp (15 to 30 mL) olive oil

1 Tbsp (15 mL) yellow mustard seeds

2 onions, finely chopped

2 garlic cloves, minced

1 tsp (5 mL) fresh ginger, finely chopped

1 Tbsp (15 mL) turmeric

1 tsp (5 mL) cardamom

1 tsp (5 mL) cumin

1 lb (500 g) cauliflower, trimmed and cut into florets

1 lb (500 g) parsnips, peeled and cut into chunks roughly the same size as the cauliflower

2 cups (500 mL) vegetable or chicken stock or water

1⅔ cups (400 mL) coconut milk

sea salt and freshly ground pepper to taste

1 Tbsp (15 mL) fresh cilantro, finely chopped

Heat the oil in a large saucepan over medium-high heat. When the oil is hot, add the mustard seeds and cook until they begin to pop. Add onion, garlic and ginger, and cook for a couple of minutes until the onion is soft and translucent. Add turmeric, cardamom and cumin. Add cauliflower and parsnip and cook the mixture while stirring for a couple of minutes. Add the stock or water to the pan and bring it slowly to a boil. Skim off any scum that comes to the top and reduce the soup to a simmer. Leave it to cook gently for 30 minutes, stirring regularly.

The soup is ready when the cauliflower is cooked and tender. Stir in the coconut milk. Purée the soup in the blender until smooth and return it to a clean saucepan. Season the soup with salt and pepper, garnish with cilantro and serve.

Tip
Parsnips are best stored in a very cold location or in the refrigerator.

For a different snack, try making parsnip chips! Peel 3 or 4 parsnips lengthwise with a sharp vegetable peeler into long paper thin strips, until you've reached the central core. Heat oil in a medium-sized saucepan to 350˚ F (175˚ C) and drop parsnip strips in small batches and fry for 1 minute until crisp and golden. Drain on paper towels, season with sea salt and serve.

Curried Pumpkin Soup

Serves 4 to 6

Friendly rivalries amongst farmers to see who could grow the largest pumpkin have no doubt been going on for hundreds of years, but it wasn't until William Warnock of Goderich sent his record-shattering 400-pound (181-kilogram) pumpkin to the 1900 World's Fair in Paris that gigantic pumpkins received world-wide attention. In 1903 Warnock broke his own record with a 403-pound (183 kilogram) pumpkin at the St. Louis World's Fair; this was a record that remained untouched until 1976! Pumpkins *(Cucurbita pepo)* and other squashes are New World plants that humans have cultivated as food crops for at least 7000 years. They were important for many First Nation peoples; the flesh was consumed raw or roasted, the flowers and seeds were sometimes eaten and the skins could be cut into strips, dried and made into mats.

splash of olive oil

2 medium yellow onions, finely chopped

2 cloves garlic, finely chopped

1 tsp (5 mL) mustard seeds

1 piece of fresh ginger, 1-inch (2.5 cm) wide, peeled and finely chopped

3 lbs (1.5 kg) sugar pumpkin, peeled, seeded and cut into bite-sized chunks

vegetable or chicken stock or water, enough to cover vegetables

1 tsp (5 mL) turmeric

1²⁄₃ cups (400 mL) coconut milk

sea salt and freshly ground pepper to taste

1 small handful of cilantro leaves, finely chopped

Heat the oil in a medium pot over medium-high heat. When the oil is hot, add the onion, garlic, mustard seeds and ginger and cook for a couple of minutes until the onion is soft and translucent. Add pumpkin chunks to the pot and cook for a couple of minutes while stirring. Add stock or water and turmeric and bring slowly to a boil. Skim off any scum that comes to the top and reduce the soup to a simmer. Cook gently for at least 20 minutes, stirring occasionally.

When the pumpkin is tender, remove from heat and purée one-third of the soup with the coconut milk in a blender or food processor. Return to the pot. Bring back to a simmer and season with salt and pepper. Serve hot, garnished with the cilantro sprinkled on top.

Pumpkins aren't the only vegetables that have been carved at Halloween. Beets and turnips have also been at the sharp end of a carver's knife, although these days it's hard to imagine a Halloween beet touching our hearts the same way a carved pumpkin does.

Chicken and Mushroom Pot Pie

Serves 4

A pot pie is a wonderful comfort food when the weather cools down in fall. This one combines chicken, which is abundant in our grocery stores year-round, and seasonal vegetables in a rich gravy. It's a good idea to seek out and buy local, organic, free-range chicken if you can—the extra flavour is worth the effort. Chicken pairs well with a multitude of flavours, and it is tasty on its own—the famous saying, "tastes like chicken," might not be such a bad analogy when you consider the diversity of this simple food. Originating in Thailand, chickens (*Gallus gallus domesticus*) were first domesticated from red junglefowl around 7000 BC. They were quickly popularized as a domestic animal throughout the world—chickens were small and inexpensive to buy and raise, and they provided a meal, either by way of the meat or the eggs.

2 Tbsp (30 mL) unsalted butter

1 medium yellow onion, finely chopped

2 carrots, peeled and diced

2 celery stalks, diced

1 tsp (5 mL) garlic, minced

¼ tsp (1 mL) sea salt

¼ tsp (1 mL) freshly ground black pepper

6 oz (170 gm) mushrooms, sliced

½ tsp (2 mL) fresh thyme, chopped

3 bay leaves

2 Tbsp (30 mL) dry sherry

¼ cup (60 mL) flour

2 cups (500 mL) chicken stock

1 cup cream (10%)

3 cups (750 mL) cooked chicken, cubed

½ cup (125 mL) peas, fresh or frozen

1 Tbsp (15 mL) parsley, chopped

Preheat the oven to 375° F (190° F). Butter an 8-cup (2 L) baking dish and set aside.

In a large pot, melt butter over medium-high heat and cook onions, carrots and celery until soft, 3 to 4 minutes. Add garlic, salt and pepper and cook, stirring, for 30 seconds. Then add mushrooms, thyme, bay leaves and cook, stirring, until the mushrooms are soft and have given off their liquid, about 3 minutes. Add sherry and cook until most of the liquid is evaporated. Stir in flour and cook, stirring, for 2 minutes. Stirring constantly, slowly add the chicken stock and cream and cook until the mixture is smooth and thickened, about 5 minutes. Add the chicken, peas and parsley, stir well, and cook until chicken is heated through. Pour filling into baking dish and set aside.

For the pastry, mix together flour, baking powder and salt in a bowl. Rub butter into the mixture using the tips of your fingers until the mixture looks like coarse crumbs. Gently fold in buttermilk until mixture just comes together. Roll out dough on a floured surface and shape to fit the top of the baking dish.

Lay pastry on top of the filling and score pastry slightly with a knife, so it is easier to cut after baking. Brush with egg and bake for 20 to 25 minutes or until crust is golden brown.

Ontario is the number one poultry producer in Canada. The average Canadian eats over 60 lb (30 kg) of chicken every year.

Pastry

2 cups (500 mL) flour

1 Tbsp (15 mL) baking powder

1/4 tsp (1 mL) sea salt

6 Tbsp (90 mL) butter, cold

¾ cup (175 mL) buttermilk

1 egg, beaten

Pumpkin Fondue

Serves 12 as an appetizer

A diverse and warming meal that was meant to be shared, the fondue was popular in Ontario in the 1970s. Just about everyone who got married during that decade received a fondue pot as a gift. Today, fondues have made a comeback as a tasty, somewhat special part of a social gathering. You can even buy fondue pots dating from the 70s at garage sales! Fondue is certainly one of the most perfect cold-weather foods. The word "fondue" comes from the French verb *fondre*, "to melt." Originating in the Swiss Alps, fondue was born of necessity during the cold months when food was scarce. By melting hard, dry cheeses in a caquelon (a traditional, small earthenware pot) and enriching them with ingredients such as wine, an almost seductive meal ensued that could transform even the stalest crust of bread. The following pumpkin fondue is quite a departure from the traditional one, but it is equally enticing.

1 sugar pumpkin, about 3 to 4 lbs (1.5 to 2 kg)

2 Tbsp (30 mL) unsalted butter

1 small onion, finely chopped

1 clove garlic, minced

1 cup (250 mL) dry white wine

pinch of freshly grated nutmeg

2 Tbsp (30 mL) flour

¼ cup (60 mL) fresh sage, chopped

2 cups (500 mL) grated aged white cheddar cheese

½ cup (125 mL) sour cream

sea salt and freshly ground pepper to taste

Preheat oven to 350° F (175° C). Pierce the top of the pumpkin with a knife 3 or 4 times, and bake for 20 minutes. Let cool for 10 minutes. Remove top a quarter of the way down, forming a lid. Scoop out the seeds and fibres and set aside. Increase oven temperature to 375° F (190° C).

Melt butter in a medium saucepan and sauté onion for 5 minutes. Add garlic and cook until softened. Add white wine and bring to a simmer. Finally, add nutmeg, flour, sage and cheddar cheese and stir until the cheese is melted. Pour into the pumpkin, cover with its lid and bake for 20 minutes, until the mixture is hot. Remove from oven and stir in sour cream. Adjust salt and pepper, if needed, and serve with skewers of crusty bread for dipping and spoons for scooping out the delicious pumpkin flesh.

Apple-roasted Pheasant

Serves 4

The ringed-necked pheasant *(Phasianus colchicus)* is a popular upland game bird introduced to Ontario in 1895. It proved a good match to the landscape but as hunting demands grew, pen-raised birds were released in greater and greater numbers, eventually depleting wild stocks. In 2003 a plan to reintroduce wild ring-necked pheasants into Ontario began with help from a hardy stock from southern Saskatchewan and the hopes that a true Ontario strain of wild pheasant will soon emerge. Flintshire Farms, North America's largest integrated pheasant farm, is located in Flinton. Since 1977 the company has provided Ontarians with free-range pheasant meats and products. They have even developed an all-white breed of pheasant, aptly called the Flintshire white pheasant.

4 pheasant breasts, skin on, wing attached

sea salt and freshly cracked black pepper

1 Tbsp (15 mL) butter

1 Tbsp (15 mL) grape seed oil or olive oil

4 cups (32 oz) Pink Lady apples, peeled and sliced

¼ cup (60 mL) honey

1 Tbsp (15 mL) garlic, minced

1 tsp (5 mL) cinnamon

1 tsp (5 mL) cloves

juice of half a lemon

Preheat oven to 425° F (220° C). Season pheasant with salt and pepper. Heat butter and oil in an ovenproof sauté pan that is large enough to comfortably fit all the meat. On medium-high heat, sear pheasant breasts, skin side down, for 3 to 4 minutes until golden brown. Set aside.

Combine all the remaining ingredients in a mixing bowl and sauté in the same pan as the pheasant. When the apples are nicely caramelized, about 5 minutes, place the pheasant on top, skin sides up, and roast in the oven for 10 to 12 minutes, until the meat is cooked through.

Serve the breasts atop a spoonful of the caramelized apples.

Native to Japan and China, the pheasant is a member of the Phasianidae family of birds, which includes the quail and the peacock. Terrestrial birds that can be distinguished by the male's ornate plumage, pheasants were introduced into North America in 1881.

Macadamia-roasted Pork with Maple Syrup

Serves 8 to 10

Pork is a lean, high-quality protein source and today is much lower in fat than it has ever been. In fact, the same size serving of pork tenderloin and chicken breast contain the same amount of fat. In Canada, pork was the first meat to play an important economic role, and by the 1850s, pork products, especially bacon, were being regularly exported to Britain. In 1874 Canada's first large-scale pork processing facility was built in Toronto. Today, Canada produces about 30 million pigs per year, and is the world's largest pork exporter—50 percent of our pork is exported to over 85 countries. Ontario, with about 4000 farms, is the country's second-largest pork producer after Quebec. In Canada, 98 percent of pig farms are family owned and operated.

Stuffing

2 Tbsp (30 mL) olive oil

1 onion, finely chopped

4 cloves garlic, roughly chopped

¼ cup (60 mL) fresh rosemary, chopped

¼ cup (60 mL) fresh thyme, chopped

2 cups (500 mL) macadamia nuts, roughly chopped

¼ cup (60 mL) chicken stock

2 Tbsp (30 mL) dry bread crumbs

1 Tbsp (15 mL) dark brown sugar

2 x 3 lb (1.4 kg) pork loin rib roast, patted dry, room temperature

sea salt and freshly ground pepper

butcher twine

3 to 6 sprigs of fresh rosemary

1 Tbsp (15 mL) olive oil

Glaze

½ cup (125 mL) maple syrup

¼ cup (60 mL) white wine, preferably a Riesling

¼ cup (60 mL) chicken broth

sea salt and freshly ground pepper

Preheat oven to 400° F (200° C). Heat olive oil in a pan and cook onions, garlic, rosemary and thyme a few minutes. Add macadamia nuts. Stir in chicken stock, bread crumbs and brown sugar, and set stuffing aside.

Turn the pork loin rib roast fat side down. Slit lengthwise, almost but not quite all the way through, to form a long pocket, leaving a ½ inch (1 cm) border of uncut meat at each end. Sprinkle generously with salt and pepper. Fill the cavity with the stuffing. Tie loin together with butcher twine or heavy duty kitchen string at 1½ inch (3 to 4 cm) intervals. Slide the rosemary sprigs under the twine. Brush with remaining olive oil and sprinkle generously with salt and pepper. Set, fat side up, diagonally or curved (so it fits) on a large baking sheet or jelly roll pan.

Mix maple syrup, white wine and chicken broth together. Brush glaze mixture on meat.

Roast in the oven until a meat thermometer registers 150 to 155° F (65 to 68° C), about 2 hours, occasionally brushing with the pan drippings. Let roast rest 15 to 20 minutes out of the oven, then transfer to a carving board.

To make the sauce, stir juices around pan to loosen browned bits. Pour through a strainer into a small pan, and stir in port and chicken stock. Bring to simmer and cook until lightly thickened. Slice pork roast and serve with sauce.

Sauce
¼ cup (60 mL) port
¼ cup (60 mL) chicken stock

Duck Confit with Caramelized Rutabaga and Risotto

Serves 10

Scientists believe that rutabagas have the extra benefit of being cancer fighters. Over 55 million pounds of rutabagas are grown in Ontario—considered a small crop—but the majority stays within the province. Believed to be a hybrid of a turnip and a cabbage, the rutabaga (*Brassica napus* var. *napobrassica*) has an earthy, sweet flavour and creamy flesh. It first became popular in 17th-century Sweden, and in Australia, New Zealand and the United Kingdom, it is still known as a "swede." The name "rutabaga" comes from the Swedish word *rotabagge,* which means "baggy root." In this recipe, the rutabagas are caramelized to bring out their sweetness in the risotto, a slow-cooked rice dish of Italian origin.

10 duck legs

2 heads garlic, halved crosswise

1 lemon, sliced into about 5 rings

1 orange, sliced into about 5 rings

½ cinnamon stick

4 star anise, whole

1 tsp (5 mL) black peppercorns, whole

½ inch (1 cm) fresh ginger, sliced into three pieces

6 sprigs of fresh thyme

3 bay leaves

½ lb (250g) kosher salt

about 2 lbs (1 kg) of rendered duck fat and 4 cups (1 L) grape seed or olive oil

Rutabaga

2 Tbsp (30 mL) butter

2 Tbsp (30 mL) brown sugar

2 small rutabaga, peeled, quartered and sliced, ¼ inch thick

sea salt and freshly ground pepper to taste

Layer the duck legs, garlic halves, lemon and orange slices, spices and herbs, in a nonreactive container, generously sprinkling with salt between each layer. Cover with plastic wrap, and cure in refrigerator for 24 hours.

Preheat the oven to 250˚ F (120˚ C). Remove the duck legs and pat them dry (you can rinse them if you prefer a milder salt flavour). Rinse and drain garlic, fruit, spices and herbs. Place duck legs and fruit mixture, alternating layers, into a deep baking dish and cover with the duck fat and oil. Bake for 6 to 8 hours or until the meat is very tender. The duck is ready to serve hot or it can be cooled and preserved in a crock or plastic container in the refrigerator for up to 3 months. If storing, strain the fat through a fine sieve and pour enough over the meat to cover.

To prepare the rutabaga, heat butter and brown sugar in a small pan until butter is melted. Add rutabaga slices and cook over medium heat until tender, about 12 to 15 minutes. Season with salt and pepper and set aside.

For the risotto, melt butter in a skillet over medium heat and sauté onion until softened but not coloured, about 5 minutes. Add the rice and sauté for 2 to 4 minutes, stirring to coat the grains. Then add the white wine, stir to combine until it is absorbed, about 3 minutes. Add a ladle of the hot broth, stirring slowly but continuously, until it is almost completely absorbed by the rice. Continue adding broth until all of it is absorbed and the rice is tender but slightly chewy and very creamy. This will take about 25 minutes. Stir in the remaining tablespoon of butter, parsley and Parmesan cheese. Add salt and pepper to taste. Serve the risotto piping hot with the duck confit and caramelized rutabaga.

Risotto

¼ cup (60 mL) unsalted butter, plus 1 Tbsp (15 mL) to finish

¼ cup (60 mL) onion, chopped

2 cups (500 mL) Arborio rice

½ cup (125 mL) white wine

5 cups (1.25 L) hot chicken or vegetable broth

¼ cup (60 mL) parsley, chopped

½ cup (125 mL) Parmesan cheese, grated

sea salt and freshly ground pepper to taste

Chestnut and Beef Braise

Serves 6

Now synonymous with the Christmas season, chestnuts have long been an important food source for people in the Northern Hemisphere. When other foods were scarce, chestnuts were often the only source of carbohydrates, providing much-needed fuel and energy. Once the most important forest tree in southeastern Canada, the American chestnut (*Castanea dentata*) suffered near extinction from chestnut blight in the early 1900s. The Canadian Chestnut Council, working closely with organizations in the United States, is trying to recover this threatened species and important part of our history.

3 lbs (1.5 kg) inside round roast

sea salt and freshly ground pepper to taste

¼ cup (60 mL) canola or sunflower oil

1 cup (250 mL) red wine, preferably Pinot Noir

2 cups (500 mL) beef stock

1 clove garlic, crushed with a heavy knife

2 fresh Roma tomatoes, quartered

2 cups (500 mL) baby carrots

2 cups (500 mL) pearl onions

2 cups (500 mL) small white mushrooms

1 x 10 oz (283 g) jar chestnuts, drained and roughly chopped

Preheat oven to 350° F (175° C). Season meat well with salt and pepper. Heat the oil in a Dutch oven and brown the meat; remove from pan. Add red wine and bring to a rapid boil on high heat until liquid is reduced and any drippings are loosened from the bottom of the pot. Add the beef stock and stir. Return the roast to the pan and add remaining ingredients. Cover and cook in the oven until tender, about 1½ hours, turning occasionally.

Remove the meat from the pan and strain out the liquid, reserving vegetables. Reduce the sauce until thickened. Season to taste.

Place the meat on a serving dish and add reserved vegetables. Serve with the sauce and roasted potatoes.

Braising is a technique in which a tougher cut of beef—chuck, round or brisket—is slowly cooked with vegetables in liquid so that it becomes tender.

Pappardelle with Black Winter Truffles

Serves 4

Seductive and intense, French black truffles *(Tuber melanosporum)* are the world's most precious tubers. They are related to mushrooms but differ in many ways—the most obvious difference is that they grow underground. Often called "the perfume of the earth itself," the truffle is a coveted aphrodisiac, strongly scented with a musky earthiness that is evocative of sex and mystery. Truffles date back to antiquity, with a history that saw them both revered and loathed. Most truffles are harvested in late fall or winter. You can occasionally find fresh truffles at specialty markets across the province or via the Internet, but they will cost a pretty penny. You can more easily find intoxicating truffle products such as truffle butter, versatile truffle oil or even flash-frozen truffles, giving you the pleasure of the flavour at a reasonable cost.

Cream Sauce

- 1 Tbsp (15 mL) butter
- ¼ cup (60 mL) onion, finely chopped
- ½ cup (125 mL) white wine
- ½ cup (125 mL) heavy cream (32%)
- sea salt and freshly ground pepper
- ¼ cup (60 mL) grated Parmesan cheese

- 1 lb (500 g) fresh pappardelle, homemade (see next page) or store-bought
- 1 medium black winter truffle, grated, sliced or shaved

Melt butter in a skillet and sauté onion until soft. Add white wine and simmer until half the liquid is reduced. Stir in cream and simmer for 5 minutes. Season with salt and pepper.

Bring a large pot of salted water to a boil, add the pappardelle and cook until al dente, for about 5 minutes. Drain and transfer pasta to the skillet with the cream sauce and add Parmesan cheese. Toss gently to mix and transfer to a warm serving bowl. Grate fresh truffle over pasta and serve.

Tip
Have a pot of boiling water ready first, and you can prepare the sauce and cook the pasta at the same time.

Homemade Pasta

Mix flour and eggs on low speed in a heavy-duty electric mixer until mixture has a coarse, crumbly look, like corn meal. Add water in small quantities until the mixture starts to hold together. Switch to the dough hook on the mixer, or knead by hand 7 to 10 minutes. Dough should not be sticky or in separate pieces. Add a little more liquid if needed, or a little more flour if sticky. Cover with plastic wrap and let dough rest 15 to 30 minutes. Roll through a pasta machine according to the manufacturer's instructions.

To cook, make sure water is at a full boil and very well salted. Fresh pasta cooks very quickly and will rise to the top of the water when done. Drain in a colander and do not rinse.

1½ cups (375 mL) semolina flour

2 eggs

2 to 3 tsp (10 to 15 mL) lukewarm water

Steamed Artichokes with Lemon Butter

Serves 4

Recipes calling for artichokes refer to the globe artichoke (*Cynara scolymus*), which was brought to North America by French and Spanish immigrants. The artichoke, a perennial thistle, was first cultivated in Naples in the 15th century and has long been considered an aphrodisiac. Zeus fell in love with a mortal beauty named Cynara and, when she angered him, he threw her back to earth as the thorny artichoke. In early Greek and Roman times, artichokes were reputed to have a sexual power and were reserved for consumption only by men. Much later, in 1947, the yet-unknown Marilyn Monroe was named "Miss California Artichoke Queen"—no doubt a sign of things to come. In Ontario, the Gorzos family of Holland Marsh were the province's first commercial growers of artichokes; their produce is available in specialty markets. Southern Ontario gardeners can grow their own, no vegetable patch required. These plants will make a bold and striking statement when included in a sunny flowerbed.

4 smallish globe artichokes

1 clove garlic, minced, finely chopped

1 bay leaf

zest and juice from 2 lemons

¼ cup (60 mL) vegetable stock

¼ cup (60 mL) white wine

½ lb (250 g) butter

Use scissors to trim the thorny tips from the artichokes and trim off top, about ⅓ inch (0.8 cm). Steam, stem end up, in a basket over water with garlic, bay leaf and lemon zest. Cook 30 to 35 minutes or until tender. Heat the vegetable stock and white wine in a medium pan and reduce to about 2 Tbsp (30 mL).

Meanwhile, cut the butter into cubes. When the stock has reduced, lower the heat and whisk the butter in 1 cube at a time until you have used all the butter and the sauce is thick. Stir in lemon juice to taste. Place the butter sauce over low heat, being careful not to let it boil. Serve the warm artichokes with the butter sauce as an appetizer.

Tip
To prevent discolouration through oxidation, sprinkle or rub the cut surfaces of artichokes with lemon juice.

Tip
Artichokes are also available canned and frozen, and you can jazz up a home-made pizza by including them as a topping.

Cauliflower and Potato Gratin

Serves 6 to 8

Cauliflower is a member of the mustard family, and like most of this family's members, it is a cool climate crop. It grows best in regions where summers aren't too hot. Though it can seem hard to believe on a hot, humid summer day in July, Ontario is one of these places. This frost-resistant crop can be planted quite early in spring, is often ready for harvest as early as June and lasts through September. Fused with cheese and buttery cream, cauliflower and Yukon Gold potatoes work well in this hearty dish.

1½ cups (375 mL) Gruyere cheese, grated

½ cup (125 mL) Parmesan cheese, grated

1 Tbsp (15 mL) butter

1 medium onion, diced

2 cloves garlic, minced

2 cups (500 mL) heavy cream (32%)

1 tsp (5 mL) freshly grated nutmeg

4 lbs (2 kg) Yukon Gold potatoes, peeled and thinly sliced

2 medium cauliflower, sliced ¼ inch (.5 cm) thick

sea salt and freshly ground pepper

¼ cup (60 mL) fresh thyme, chopped

Butter an 8-cup (2 L) shallow baking dish and preheat the oven to 350° F (175° C). Combine the cheeses, reserving ½ cup (125 mL) for the topping and put aside. Sauté the onions in the butter until soft, add the garlic and cook for 2 minutes. Add the cream, bring just to the boil and remove from the heat. Stir in the nutmeg. Layer the potatoes and cauliflower in the baking dish, seasoning each layer with salt and pepper and thyme and a sprinkle of the cheeses. Continue layering until you have used all the potatoes and cauliflower, and pour the cream over the vegetables. Top with the reserved cheese, cover and bake for 35 to 40 minutes or until the vegetables are tender. Remove the cover and continue cooking until the top is golden brown, about 10 more minutes. Let rest at least 10 minutes or up to ½ hour before serving.

Gratins can be made with vegetables such as zucchini, winter squash, tomatoes and leeks. They make a perfect meal together with some crusty French bread.

Roasted Jerusalem Artichokes

Serves 4

Also known as "sunchoke" and "Canada potato," the Jerusalem artichoke *(Helianthus tuberosus)* is a tuber native to North America. Its flesh is waxy, and the texture is reminiscent of crispy apple and sunflower seeds. Traditionally, Jerusalem artichoke tubers were simply boiled and eaten much like potatoes, and they can be used in place of potatoes in many recipes. The first written record of this edible member of the sunflower family was in 1603, when Samuel de Champlain encountered it growing in the vegetable gardens of First Nations peoples. Today, Jerusalem artichokes do not carry the same clout they once had. Other than occasionally being marketed as a specialty vegetable, most farmers in Ontario consider them a weed and a nuisance. Jerusalem artichokes are very easy to grow and, with enough sunshine, produce a cheery display of small sunflowers late in the year.

4 cloves garlic, chopped

2½ Tbsp (37 mL) extra virgin olive oil

1½ lbs (750 g) Jerusalem artichokes

sea salt and freshly ground black pepper to taste

1 Tbsp (15 mL) chopped fresh parsley

Preheat oven to 350° F (175° C). Heat garlic and oil in a small pot and cook until soft. Peel Jerusalem artichokes and cut into small chunks, placing chunks into a bowl of acidulated water (see next page) as you work. Put in a shallow roasting pan large enough to hold everything in one layer comfortably. Strain garlic from oil and pour oil over the chokes. Add salt and pepper and toss.

Bake in oven for about 20 minutes, stirring once or twice, until tender. Sprinkle parsley on top and serve as a side dish.

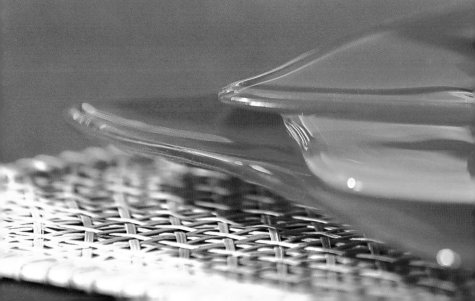

The Jerusalem artichoke has no ties to the famous Biblical city; the name simply comes from the English misunderstanding of the Italian word girasol, *which means "sunflower."*

Acidulated water is just water to which a little acid—normally lemon or lime juice or vinegar—has been added; ½ tsp (2 mL) per cup (250 mL) is enough. When you are peeling or cutting fruits or vegetables that discolour quickly when exposed to air, like apples, place them in acidulated water to prevent browning. Jerusalem artichokes, globe artichokes and salsify are just some of the foods that benefit from this treatment. Acidulated water is also sometimes used for cooking.

Pancetta and Pine Nut Brussels Sprouts

Serves 6

Brussels sprouts (*Brassica oleracea* var. *gemmifera*) originally hail from the area around Afghanistan and they are, like cauliflower, actually a variety of cabbage. They were reputedly first cultivated in large quantities in Belgium, hence the name. Because they do well in cool climates, Brussels sprouts are perfectly suited to Ontario; they even improve in flavour, sweetness and tenderness if allowed to chill through a few frosts. They are often available at farmers' markets, where they are often sold still attached to the stem. Brussels sprouts are most often over-cooked, which is a regrettable practice that releases the sprouts' naturally occurring sulphur, giving them a pungent smell and taste. When properly cooked—especially if given an opportunity to "ripen" during a frost—this vegetable is sweet and nutty, and it provides many nutritional benefits, such as vitamins, folic acid and dietary fibre.

2 lbs (1 kg) Brussels sprouts

splash of olive oil

5 oz (140 g) pancetta, diced

sea salt and freshly ground pepper to taste

½ cup (125 mL) pine nuts, toasted

Preheat oven to 400° F (200° C). Slice the Brussels sprouts in half lengthwise, removing any loose, outer leaves and trimming the bottom stems. Toss in olive oil and add pancetta, salt and pepper. Spread in a single layer on a baking sheet and bake for 20 to 30 minutes until pancetta is crispy. Stir occasionally, so the Brussels sprouts cook evenly. Toss with the pine nuts and another splash of olive oil, if desired.

Tip
To toast pine nuts, place in a dry frying pan and cook on low heat, stirring occasionally until lightly golden.

Pancetta is Italian bacon and is available at most delis and Italian markets.

Maple Candied Sweet Potatoes

Serves 4 to 6

Another indigenous tuber, the sweet potato (*Ipomoea batatas*), is a traditional accompaniment to Thanksgiving dinner. Probably dating back to Peru as early as 8000 BC, the sweet potato is often confused with the yam, a vegetable native to West Africa. A member of the magnolia family, the sweet potato is only distantly related to the potato. Although not commonly eaten, the leaves and shoots of the sweet potato plant are also edible and make an interesting addition to salads. The most popular sweet potato varieties in Ontario are "Garnet" and "Jewel," which do well in our northern climate. They are extra sweet and have striking orange flesh.

1 cup (250 mL) maple syrup

1 cup (250 mL) orange juice

½ cup (125 mL) fresh lime juice

½ cup (125 mL) water

¼ cup (60 mL) melted butter

3 lbs (1.5 kg) sweet potatoes

Combine maple syrup, fruit juices and water in a nonreactive saucepan large enough to hold all the sweet potatoes comfortably. Bring to a boil, then reduce to a simmer.

Peel the sweet potatoes, slicing the longer ones in half, and place in the saucepan. Cook, turning occasionally, for about one and a half hours, or until the edges of the sweet potatoes turn slightly translucent and they are tender.

Transfer onto a serving platter and drizzle with the melted butter.

Ipomoea batatas or sweet potato vine is a vigorous, twining, climbing annual that is grown in containers for its attractive foliage rather than its flowers.

Creamy Espresso Martini

Serves 1

Coffee (*Coffea* species) was discovered in Ethiopia, legend has it, by a farmer who noticed his goat's boisterous behaviour after eating some berries. Only when the berries (they are actually seeds, not beans) reached Turkey in the 15th century were they roasted and crushed to make an early version of today's beverage. The coffee industry today employs an astounding 20 million people worldwide and is second in value only to petroleum products in international trade. The average coffee drinker consumes three cups per day, and about a third of all retail sales of coffee in Canada are made in Ontario.

1 oz (30 mL) cold espresso

1½ oz (45 mL) vodka, coffee or vanilla flavour

1½ oz (45 mL) coffee liqueur

1 oz (30 mL) Irish cream liqueur

1 scoop (¼ cup [60 mL]) vanilla ice cream

Pour ingredients into a shaker and shake vigorously. Strain into a chilled martini glass.

Coffee is the most popular beverage worldwide, owing to its caffeine content and flavour. But did you know that most people employed to grow and harvest coffee beans live well below the poverty line and are not paid a fair price for their labour? Considering the multi-billion dollar profit the coffee industry boasts, we recommend you seek out and purchase Fair Trade and organically grown coffee so that you may enjoy your java guilt-free.

Caramel-dipped Apples

Serves 8

Early French settlers likely planted the first apples (*Malus domestica*) in what is now Canada in and around Port Royal in the early 1600s. In 1811 John McIntosh (1777–1845) discovered about 20 apple trees growing in a wooded area of his farm, near what is now Prescott, Ontario. He transplanted some of them, and one of the transplants produced a fruit he considered superior. His son Allen was instrumental in the apple's spread, through teaching many surrounding farmers how to reproduce the delicious fruit tree using grafting and budding techniques. The original McIntosh apple tree lived for over 90 years and was left standing to commemorate the hard work and dedication of the McIntosh family. Apples are Canada's largest fruit crop, and the McIntosh—the only variety grown in all apple-growing regions of Canada—makes up half of all Canadian apple production. Macs are excellent raw or in pies, cakes, crisps, butters and ciders—one a day to keep the doctor away!

1 lb (500 g) dark brown sugar

¾ cup (175 mL) unsalted butter, room temperature

1 x 10 oz (300 mL) can sweetened condensed milk

⅔ cup (150 mL) light corn syrup

1/4 tsp (1 mL) sea salt

1 tsp (5 mL) vanilla

¼ cup (60 mL) whipping cream

8 apples, such as McIntosh or Granny Smith, stems removed, washed and dried

8 wooden sticks such as craft sticks, popsicle sticks or even chopsticks

Combine brown sugar, butter, condensed milk, corn syrup and salt in a heavy-bottomed pot over medium-low heat and stir slowly but continually to dissolve sugar until it reaches a temperature between 234° F and 240° F (112° C and 115° C) on a candy thermometer, or the soft-ball stage (see opposite). Remove from heat, stir in vanilla and whipping cream and pour into a clean metal bowl. Cool until caramel is 200° F (95° C), about 15 minutes.

While caramel is cooling, line a baking sheet with buttered parchment paper and push one stick into the stem end of each apple. Dip apples in caramel and let excess caramel drip off before setting on the greased paper. Cool before eating and chill any uneaten apples, wrapped in cellophane, up to 1 week.

Tip

If your apples are quite waxy, dip them in boiling water for 30 seconds to remove the wax, and dry very well.

Tip

Once the caramel apples have set, dip them into melted chocolate for an extra decadent Halloween treat. You can also roll them in chopped nuts, candy sprinkles or crushed candy bars!

Tip
The soft-ball stage is a candy test where you drop a little syrup in cold water, and as the syrup cools, it forms a soft ball that flattens when it is removed from the water.

Cucumber and Fresh Dill Salad

Serves 6

Cucumbers are Ontario's second largest hothouse crop after tomatoes, making them a refreshing and local treat that is available year-round. Garden-grown cucumbers are ready to be harvested in Ontario from June to October. The cucumber (*Cucumis sativa*) was first cultivated in India over 3000 years ago. Cucumbers are members of the squash family, which, along with corn and beans, formed the famous "Three Sisters" of early Native American cuisine. In 1535, Jacques Cartier found "very great cucumbers" growing in what is now Montréal. Because cucumbers are 95 percent water, they are not especially packed with nutrition, but they are a good source of vitamins C and K, silica and potassium. This water-rich, refreshing fruit can also be enjoyed in the heat of summer to keep you feeling as "cool as a cucumber." Fresh dill is available year-round in most supermarkets. For summer use, you can easily grow both dill and cucumbers in your garden.

4 large, long English cucumbers

1 medium red onion, halved and thinly sliced

1 bunch fresh dill, finely chopped, about 1 cup (250 mL)

¼ cup (60 mL) cider vinegar

1 to 2 Tbsp (15 to 30 mL) honey, to taste

1 cup (250 ml) sour cream or plain yogurt

sea salt and freshly ground pepper to taste

Wash the cucumbers and peel in lengthwise strips, being sure to leave a bit of dark green skin between each strip. Thinly slice, and place slices, along with the onion and fresh dill, in a large glass bowl.

In a separate, small bowl, make a dressing with the vinegar, honey, sour cream, salt and pepper. Add dressing to large bowl and mix well to combine.

Allow the salad to sit for at least 15 minutes before serving as a side dish.

Although considered a vegetable, cucumbers are actually the fruit of the cucumber plant, which belongs to the same family of plants as melons and pumpkins.

Mixed Citrus Salad with Lemongrass Vinaigrette

Serves 4

Oranges, lemons and limes originated as wild fruit in Southeast Asia thousands of years ago. Their taste, colour and fragrance made them very popular, and many cultures contributed to their spread across the globe. Today, citrus fruits are cultivated in about 140 countries, with about half of the total production dedicated to oranges. Citrus fruits are particularly popular and much appreciated in winter because of their long shelf life and refreshing, bright taste. And we can't forget the long-anticipated Christmas oranges (mandarins, clementines, satsumas), with their easy-to-peel skin and super sweet taste. They have surely become as much a part of an Ontario Christmas as snow and St. Nick.

2 large grapefruit, peeled, and segmented

2 oranges, peeled and segmented

2 blood oranges, peeled and segmented

½ cup (125 mL) kumquats, sliced in thin rounds

1 star fruit, sliced crosswise

handful of fresh mint, chopped

Dressing

1 stalk lemongrass, tender bottom only

½ cup (125 mL) apple juice

2 Tbsp (30 mL) honey or agave syrup

1 Tbsp (15 mL) shallots, finely chopped

zest and juice from 1 lime

2 Tbsp (30 mL) canola or sunflower oil

Combine the fruit in a medium-sized bowl and let sit for 15 minutes.

For the dressing, bruise and roughly chop the lemongrass. In a small saucepan, combine apple juice, honey or agave syrup, lemongrass. Bring to a boil and cook for 5 minutes. Remove saucepan from heat and let cool to room temperature. Add shallots, lime zest and juice and oil, and whisk together until well blended.

Toss citrus fruit and mint with dressing and serve.

Oranges were named not for their colour but for their scent. The word "orange" comes from the Sanskrit naranga, *which means "fragrant.*

Potato and Roasted Garlic Chowder

Serves 4

Roasted garlic has a smooth, buttery flavour that is very different from fresh garlic and adds a subtle nuance to this chowder. Garlic is grown in Ontario commercially, and you can grow it in a home garden or planter. Since 1997 Perth has promoted Ontario-grown garlic with its annual garlic festival. Sudbury, Stratford and Ottawa have similar celebrations of the 'stinking rose' in August. Farmers' markets throughout the province are the best source for the freshest, best quality garlic.

2 medium onions, diced

¼ cup (60 mL) unsalted butter

1 Tbsp (15 mL) olive oil

2 cups (500 mL) celery, diced

1 cup (250 mL) carrots, diced

4 medium potatoes, peeled and diced

1 bay leaf

vegetable or chicken stock, enough to just cover vegetables

2 bulbs roasted garlic (see next page), cloves squeezed out and roughly chopped

2 cups (500 ml) heavy cream (32%)

sea salt and freshly ground pepper to taste

¼ cup (60 ml) fresh herbs such as parsley, thyme or mint, chopped

In a heavy pot, sauté the onions in the butter and oil until they turn golden. Add the vegetables, bay leaf and cover with stock. Simmer for 15 minutes, then add the roasted garlic and cream, and simmer for 10 to 15 minutes more or until the potatoes are cooked and the soup is reduced and creamy. Season to taste with salt and pepper. Ladle soup into bowls and garnish with a sprinkle of herbs.

Roasted Garlic

You can roast as little or as much garlic as you want. I tend to roast 5 or 6 bulbs at a time, so I will have leftovers to last a week. Preheat the oven to 350° F (175° C). Slice the top of each bulb of garlic to expose the cloves, and lay them cut side up in a baking dish. Drizzle with olive oil and sprinkle with sea salt. Roast 20 to 30 minutes or until cloves are tender. Remove from oven and set aside until cool enough to handle. The buttery flesh of the cloves will come out of the bulb easily when you squeeze it (throw out the papery skin of the bulb). Alternatively, you can serve the whole roasted bulbs as a garnish to grilled meats or vegetables.

Muskoka Ale and Cheddar Soup

Serves 4

Over the past decade, many microbrewers and artisan brewers have emerged throughout Canada, offering superior, small-batch beers to connoisseurs. Before Prohibition, which reached its peak in Canada in the early 1920s, small craft breweries were the norm. The resurgence of Canadian independent brewing didn't start until the 1980s; it is credited in large part to Ontarian Jim Brickman, who opened the first post-Prohibition craft brewery in the province. Today in Ontario about 30 craft breweries produce over 130 beers. Ales are a very common type of beer in all of Canada's eastern provinces, usually brewed using barley. This soup works well with a cream ale such as award-winning Muskoka Cream Ale, because of its fruity flavour and buttery finish.

2 medium onions, diced

1 Tbsp (15 ml) olive oil

¼ cup (60 ml) unsalted butter

2 cups (500 ml) celery, diced

1 cup (250 ml) parsnips, diced

4 medium potatoes, peeled and diced

1 bay leaf

vegetable or chicken stock, enough to just cover vegetables

2 cups (500 ml) heavy cream (32%)

2 cups (500 mL) sharp white Cheddar cheese, grated

½ to 1 bottle of Muskoka Cream Ale, about 6 to 12 oz (170 to 341 mL) or to taste

sea salt and freshly ground pepper

In a heavy pot, sauté the onions in the butter and oil until they turn golden. Add celery, parsnips, potatoes, bay leaf and add enough stock to cover everything. Simmer for 15 minutes, then add the cream and simmer for 10 to 15 minutes more or until the potatoes are cooked and the soup is reduced and creamy. Remove soup from heat and blend in cheese in small batches. Return to medium-low heat and stir in ale to taste. Season with salt and pepper and serve.

Canadians spend over 6.7 billion dollars per year on beer, accounting for more than 51 percent of the sales of all alcohol combined.

Cioppino with Fennel and Saffron

Serves 6

Cioppino is an Italian dish similar to chowder and bouillabaisse. It probably originated in the San Francisco Bay area when Italian immigrants from Genoa replaced traditional Genoese ingredients with the fresh fish available to them on the West Coast. Most Italians who came to Canada before World War II came by way of the United States. They brought with them cioppino, which means "fish stew" in the Genoese dialect. Today, Ontario's large Italian community makes up more than 80 percent of Canada's Italian population, and Italian cuisine has touched almost every corner of the province. Is there anyone out there who hasn't eaten pizza or spaghetti?

2 lbs (1 kg) snapper or swordfish fillet, cleaned

1 lb (500 g) fresh shrimp, tails on

½ lb (250 g) each clams, mussels and scallops

1 crab, cooked, cleaned and cracked

2 Tbsp (30 mL) extra virgin olive oil

1 small onion, minced

1 medium fennel bulb, diced

1 cup (250 mL) white wine

3 cloves garlic, minced

zest from half an orange, minced

pinch of saffron, or to taste, dissolved in ¼ cup (60 mL) warm stock

4 cups (1 L) tomato sauce

3 cups (750 mL) fish stock

sea salt and freshly ground pepper

½ cup (125 mL) freshly sliced basil for garnish

Wash all fish and seafood, except crab, and pat dry. In a heavy-bottomed pot, heat oil and sauté onion. Stir in fennel and sauté for 5 minutes. Add wine and garlic, and simmer for 10 minutes. Stir in orange zest, saffron, tomato sauce and stock, and simmer for 10 minutes. Nestle fish fillets and seafood into the sauce, making sure to cover them with liquid. Cover, bring back to a simmer over medium-high heat and cook until clams and mussels open, about 10 to 12 minutes. Season with salt and pepper. Serve hot in warmed bowls, garnished with fresh basil.

Tip
It is traditional to serve cioppino with polenta and a bottle of Chianti.

Note
If you have trouble finding polenta and mascarpone, try an Italian deli.

Polenta with Mascarpone

Bring milk and cream to a boil. Whisk in polenta and cook, stirring continuously, for 20 minutes. Season to taste with salt and pepper. Serve hot topped with mascarpone. You can also pour polenta into a rectangular baking dish. Once cooled, it can be sliced and pan-grilled with butter.

4 cups (1 L) milk

½ cup (125 mL) heavy cream (32%)

1 cup (250 mL) polenta

sea salt and freshly ground pepper to taste

1 cup (250 mL) mascarpone

Grilled Quail with Pistachio and Pomegranate

Serves 4

The Northern Bobwhite, a member of the quail family, has a range from southeastern Ontario all the way to Central America—in fact, it's the only native member of the family in eastern North America. Quail is considered an upland game bird, and it was part of the wild bird population of ducks, geese, grouse, partridge, turkey and pheasants that sustained the Native peoples and early settlers in the province. Quail is offered on the menus of fancy restaurants, but it is also available for the home cook in specialty shops and meat markets in many places across the province.

4 quail, cut through backbone and flattened out

sea salt and freshly ground pepper

Marinade

½ garlic clove, minced

1 tsp (5 mL) cinnamon

1 tsp (5 mL) cumin

½ onion, finely chopped

3 Tbsp (45 mL) pomegranate molasses

juice from half a lime

Sauce

1 cup (250 mL) boar bacon, diced

½ garlic clove, minced

¼ cup (60 mL) pomegranate molasses

½ cup (125 mL) pistachios, whole

sea salt and freshly ground pepper to taste

Garnish
Arugula leaves

In a large bowl, prepare marinade and toss to combine. Season each quail with salt and pepper and place in marinade. Cover and refrigerate for at least 1 hour and up to 24 hours.

For the sauce, sauté bacon in a pan until crispy. Remove all the fat drippings except for 1 Tbsp (15 mL). Add remaining ingredients and heat through.

Grill quail over medium-high heat for about 7 minutes each side, or until juices run clear.

Serve on a bed of arugula leaves with sauce drizzled on top.

Pomegranate molasses is a syrup made from cooked-down pomegranate juice. It can be found in Middle Eastern stores.

Caramelized Onion and Goat Cheese Tart

Serves 6

Because they are such great keepers, onions *(Allium cepa)* are a magnificent winter food. They are also extremely versatile and lend themselves to many uses. They can be eaten raw or cooked, chopped or whole. Introduced to North America by Columbus in 1493, they have been a prized food for thousands of years—they were often presented as gifts or even used as payment for goods or lodging. A naturally occurring antioxidant, quercetin, contributes to the reputation onions have for being very healthy. Onions grow well in our climate, and Ontario is home to many wild members of the onion family, such as wild leeks *(A. tricoccum)*, which grows in wooded areas of the province in early spring, and wild garlic *(A. vineale)*, which is most often considered a weed. Ontario is also the largest producer of commercial onions in Canada, 66 percent worth, mainly from the Holland Marsh region.

1 Tbsp (15 mL) oil

1 Tbsp (15 mL) butter

6 medium yellow onions, thinly sliced

sea salt to taste

1 tsp (5 mL) sugar

1 Tbsp (15 mL) balsamic vinegar

Béchamel

2 Tbsp (30 mL) butter

2 Tbsp (30 mL) flour

1 cup (250 mL) milk

1 bay leaf

pinch of nutmeg

1 x ¾ lb (397 g) package frozen puff pastry, thawed

egg wash made with 1 beaten egg and a splash of water

8 oz (250 g) goat cheese

2 Tbsp (30 mL) chopped fresh herbs, such as parsley, thyme or sage (optional)

Heat oil and butter in a large pan over medium heat. Add the onions, season with salt and cook until softened, about 6 minutes. Stir in the sugar and balsamic vinegar, turn the heat to medium low and cook for 30 to 45 minutes, stirring often, until nicely caramelized.

To make the béchamel, melt the butter in a small, heavy saucepan over low heat. Add flour into melted butter and stir over low heat for 5 to 7 minutes. Slowly add milk, bay leaf and nutmeg, stirring constantly, and cook for about 10 more minutes until smooth and thick.

Preheat oven to 400° F (200° C). Roll out the pastry to ⅛ inch (.25 cm) thick and place on a rectangular baking sheet. Prick all over with a fork. Brush the outside edges, about ½ inch (1 cm), with egg wash.

Combine onions and béchamel sauce in a bowl. Crumble in goat cheese and fresh herbs, if desired, and stir to combine.

Spread onion mixture onto pastry and bake for 15 to 20 minutes until pastry is puffed and golden. Let sit 10 minutes before cutting into squares. Serve warm or at room temperature with a lightly dressed green salad and port sauce (see opposite).

In a small saucepan, combine port and stock and reduce over medium heat until thick and syrupy.

Tip

This tart is perfect for picnics, potlucks and lazy Sunday brunches. Best served at room temperature or slightly warm, it makes a great "do ahead" choice for travelling or entertaining. It also could be done in individual tart shells for easy serving.

Port Sauce

1 cup (250 mL) port

½ cup (125 mL) chicken stock

Eggplant "Haggis"

Serves 6 to 8

Fair fa' your honest, sonsie face,
Great chieftain o' the puddin'-race!

Definitely a case of love it or leave it, haggis is the national dish of Scotland, the country that provided so many immigrants to early Ontario. Traditional haggis is a mixture of sheep organs and oatmeal stuffed into a sheep's stomach, which is then boiled and served like a big sausage. It is presented with *neeps* and *tatties* (turnip and potatoes, although the turnips are what we know today as rutabagas). The much-loved Scottish poet Robert Burns (1759–96) wrote the poem *Address to a Haggis,* and he is credited with making the dish famous worldwide. Each year on January 25, many people in Ontario gather to commemorate Burns' birthday, with a reading of the poem accompanying the elaborate carving and serving of the dish. Here is a vegetarian alternative to make for Robbie Burns' day.

1 large eggplant

1 cup (250 mL) red lentils

½ tsp (2 mL) sea salt

2 cups (500 mL) water

1 Tbsp (15 mL) tomato paste

dash of hot red pepper sauce

⅓ cup (75 mL) fine grain bulgur

1 large onion, finely chopped

splash of olive oil

1 clove garlic, minced

pinch each of cumin and coriander

1 to 2 Tbsp (15 to 30 mL) fresh parsley and mint, chopped

sea salt and freshly ground pepper to taste

Preheat oven to 350° F (175° C). Bake eggplant for 15 minutes or until starting to soften. Allow to cool to room temperature then cut the top end off and, using a small knife, loosen the flesh around the inside of the eggplant. Scoop out the remaining flesh, being careful not to tear the skin. Set aside the skin for the filling. (You can save the eggplant flesh for another recipe.)

Bring lentils and salted water to a boil over high heat. Turn the heat to low and simmer until the lentils are yellow and very mushy, 20 to 30 minutes, skimming off the foam that collects on the surface as they cook. Stir in tomato paste and hot red pepper sauce to taste.

Robbie might roll over in his grave at the sight and taste of an eggplant haggis, but he no doubt would be pleased that his words have stood the test of time.

Put bulgur into a bowl and pour the hot lentil mixture over it. Stir well, cover and set aside for half an hour.

Meanwhile, in a skillet sauté onion in olive oil in medium-high heat until it starts to caramelize. Add garlic, cumin, coriander and plenty of freshly ground pepper. Cook about 2 minutes more and add to the bulgur and lentil mixture and combine very well. Add the fresh parsley and mint and season with salt and pepper, if needed.

Stuff lentil mixture into eggplant shell and place in an oiled baking dish. Bake at 350° F (175° C) for 20 to 30 minutes, until hot all the way through. Slice and serve.

Cabbage Rolls

Serves 4

Cooks love to make little packages of food for their families, and cabbage leaves lend themselves particularly well to being stuffed. These cabbage rolls are of Ukrainian origin, a nod to the 30,000 displaced persons who settled in Ontario after World War II and brought their versions of cabbage rolls, borscht and pierogies to Canadian cuisine. Because cabbage rolls appear in so many cuisines, spanning continents, languages and cultures, it is difficult to pin down their origin. Small packages of food popular in Ontario today include dolmades (Greek), samosas (Indian), calzones (Italian), cornish pasties (Scottish) and potstickers (Chinese). Whatever their cultural origin, many Ontarians have fond memories of a kitchen full of women, a sampling from each generation, making light work of what will soon become dozens and dozens of delicious little packages for an upcoming holiday meal or feast at a special gathering.

1½ cups (375 mL) rice

2 cups (500 mL) vegetable or chicken stock for rice AND 2 cups or more stock for cooking cabbage rolls

1 large onion, diced

2 cloves garlic, minced

¼ cup (60 mL) butter

1 lb (500 g) fresh brown mushrooms, sliced

¼ cup (60 mL) fresh thyme, chopped

sea salt and freshly ground pepper to taste

1 medium head cabbage

2 cups (500 mL) tomato sauce

¼ cup (60 mL) heavy cream (32%)

Put rice in a pot with 2 cups (500 mL) vegetable or chicken stock. Bring to a boil, cover and simmer 10 minutes. Let sit off heat 10 minutes.

Sauté onion and garlic in butter in a pan. Add mushrooms and cook until liquid has evaporated. Stir in thyme. Add salt and pepper, and adjust to taste.

In a large bowl, combine this filling mixture with the rice. Set aside.

I like to use savoy cabbage in this recipe, but you can use ordinary green cabbage. Freeze it for a day or two (or parboil it in a large pot) so that the leaves are soft and pliable.

Cut out core from the cabbage. Bring a large pot of water to a boil and cook cabbage, pulling off leaves as they soften. Drain leaves in a colander or on paper towels. Trim tough stems from cabbage leaves and lay the leaves flat on a work surface. Place ½ cup (125 mL) filling at base of each leaf, beginning at the thick end of the leaf. Begin rolling at this end, folding edges in as you go to make a neat roll. Place finished cabbage rolls in a casserole dish and cover tightly. Recipe can be completed to this stage up to 24 hours in advance.

Heat tomato sauce in a saucepan. Bring to a boil and add cream. Simmer for 5 minutes and adjust seasoning, if needed.

Preheat oven to 375˚ F (190˚ C). Heat the vegetable or chicken stock and pour the hot stock over cabbage rolls just enough to cover them. Bake covered for 25 to 30 minutes until heated through.

Serve with hot tomato sauce and cucumber dill salad.

Roasted Turkey

Serves 8 to 10

Wild turkeys, which are smaller and more agile flyers than domesticated turkeys, range from Central America to southern Canada. These wild turkeys were domesticated by the Mayans and remain to this day a staple ingredient in Mexican cuisine, most famously as the starring ingredient in a traditional *mole*. By the beginning of the 20th century, the wild turkey population had been entirely wiped out of the province by overhunting and loss of habitat, but organizations such as the National Wildlife Turkey Federation have helped to reestablish this large fowl. Wild turkeys are now a popular but highly regulated game bird in Ontario, the most prolific being the Eastern Wild Turkey (*Meleagris gallopavo silvestris*).

1 x 12 lb (6 kg) turkey, fresh or thawed completely, if frozen

sea salt and freshly ground pepper

1 to 2 cups (250 to 500 mL) water or chicken broth (optional)

Preheat oven to 450° F (230° C). Set turkey out at room temperature for 45 minutes. Remove neck, giblets and any fat from cavity. Rinse turkey, pat dry with paper towels and season well with lots of salt and pepper. Place in a roasting pan and roast for 1¾ to 2 hours, or until an instant-read thermometer inserted into the thickest part of the thigh reads 170° F (77° C) and the juices run clear. Check the turkey after 1 hour, and if drippings are becoming too dark, add 1 to 2 cups of water or chicken broth into the pan. Remove the roasted turkey from the oven and let it rest for at least 20 minutes before carving.

Domesticated turkey production in Ontario is an important industry, and 45 percent of all Canadian turkeys are grown here, a whopping 1350 million pounds (613 million kilograms) per year.

Tip
Roasted turkey is a tried-and-true traditional dish for the holiday season. Try it with side dishes like Pancetta and Pine Nut Brussels Sprouts (p. 112), Maple Candied Sweet Potatoes (p. 114), Cauliflower and Potato Gratin (p. 108) or Balsamic-glazed Root Vegetables (p. 148).

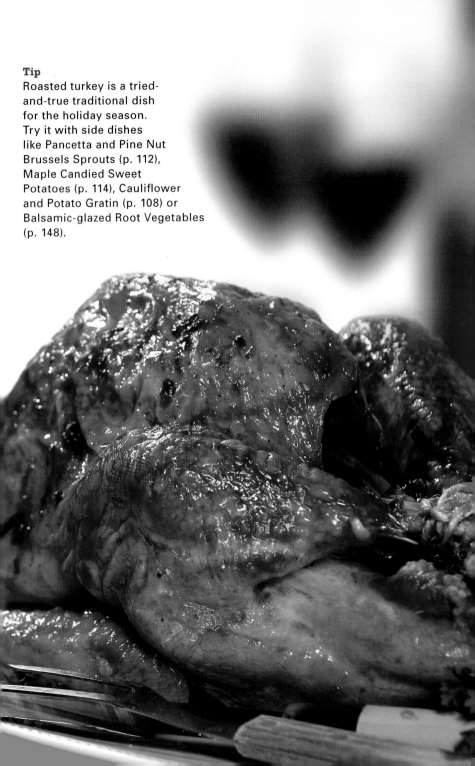

Ostrich Kabobs with Feta and Mint

Serves 6

The ostrich is a flightless bird native to Africa. Ostriches are part of the Ratite family of birds, which includes emus and rheas. These birds have been hunted and farmed for their feathers, leather and meat for a long, long time. Ostrich meat is very similar in flavour and texture to lean beef, but it is often touted as a healthier alternative because of its protein content and low fat nature. Ostriches, despite their African roots, have the uncanny ability to withstand extremes in temperature, making them a viable livestock option in our cooler climate. Ontario is home to numerous ostrich farms, such as the White Rock Ostrich Farm in Rockwood, which supplies everything ostrich, from meat and oil to guided tours of the farm. Ontario is Canada's largest producer of Ratites; Alberta comes in second.

½ cup (125 mL) feta cheese, crumbled

⅓ cup (75 mL) Kalamata olives, pitted and chopped

¼ cup (60 mL) red onion, chopped

3 Tbsp (45 mL) fresh mint leaves, finely chopped

½ tsp (2 mL) sea salt

¼ tsp (1 mL) freshly ground black pepper

1 lb (500 g) ground ostrich

In a medium bowl, combine feta cheese, olives, onion, mint, salt and pepper. Add the ostrich and lightly bring mix all the ingredients together, being careful not to overwork the mixture. Form the meat into 16 meatballs.

Thread three meatballs onto each skewer and place on a parchment-lined baking sheet, covered loosely with plastic wrap, and refrigerate for 30 minutes. Meanwhile, light the grill or preheat the broiler. Cook the kabobs for about 5 to 6 minutes per side.

Serve with warm pita bread and tzatziki.

The old and familiar tale of ostriches burying their heads in the sand at the first sign of danger is false and probably comes from early observations of these large but toothless birds eating pebbles in order to digest their food.

Placed the grated cucumber into a colander and let drain 15 minutes. Transfer grated cucumber to a bowl, squeezing out as much moisture as possible, then stir in yogurt, mint, garlic, salt and pepper. Store, refrigerated, for up to 5 days.

Tip
Wooden skewers should be soaked in water for 30 minutes before use to avoid burning.

Tzatziki

2 long English cucumbers, peeled, seeded, grated

1 cup (250 mL) plain yogurt

¼ cup (60 mL) fresh mint, chopped

1 garlic clove, minced

¼ cup (60 mL) red onion, finely diced

sea salt and freshly ground pepper to taste

White Wine and Garlic Mussels

Serves 4 to 6

Ontarians can enjoy fresh East Coast mussels throughout most of the year, but the sweetest mussel flesh is produced in the winter. Long enjoyed by coastal First Nations peoples of Canada, mussels have been actively cultivated since the 1970s to meet steadily growing consumer demand. Mussels require a great deal of care to cultivate, and they take between 18 months and two years to mature. The mussel larvae are collected from the wild and then suspended on long lines in bays along the East Coast. Plenty of fresh water and food contributes to some of the tastiest mussels available.

4 lbs (2 kg) mussels **1 cup (250 mL) white wine such as Chardonnay**	Scrub mussels under cool running water and remove any beards. Discard mussels that don't close when gently tapped.
4 garlic cloves, minced **1 Tbsp (15 mL) butter** **¼ cup (60 mL) chives, chopped**	Place white wine and garlic in a large pot and bring to a boil. Add mussels to the pot, cover and reduce heat, cooking for about 5 to 6 minutes. Discard any mussels that have not opened. With a slotted spoon transfer the mussels into serving dishes.

Turn heat to high and bring the remaining liquid to a boil. Cook for 2 to 3 minutes, until it has reduced slightly, and whisk in butter. Spoon the sauce over mussels, sprinkle with chives and serve hot.

Tip

Use your fresh mussels within 24 hours of purchasing them. The best way to store fresh mussels is to put them in a colander and place the colander into a bowl. Cover the mussels with ice and then with a damp towel. The mussels will stay very cold and have good air circulation, without being submerged (or drowned) in water.

The Zebra mussel is a fingernail-size freshwater species that has invaded the Great Lakes and St. Lawrence River systems and caused millions of dollars of damage since its discovery in Lake St. Clair in 1988.

Coq Au Vin

Serves 6

Canadian wines are earning an excellent reputation for quality within the country and abroad. In Ontario, the Niagara Peninsula is at the same latitude as Burgundy, France, with similar soil and climate, and it has recently attracted the interest of French investors. Brock University in St. Catharines boasts a world-class Cool Climate Oenology and Viticulture Institute, producing the first Canadian winemakers to learn their craft on home turf. And, of course, we cannot talk about Canadian wine without mentioning the country's crown jewel of wine, icewine. Icewine is a sweet, complex nectar of German origin that is made from fine wine grapes that have been left on the vine to freeze, thus concentrating both the sweetness and flavour. Canada, most notably Ontario, has become the world leader in icewine quality and quantity, winning countless gold medals in competitions across the globe.

2 Tbsp (30 mL) unsalted butter

⅔ cup (150 mL) boar bacon, diced

1 free-range chicken,
3 to 4 lbs (1.5 to 2 kg)
cut into 8 pieces

2 medium onions, chopped

1 carrot, chopped

1 cup (250 mL) celery root, diced

2 garlic cloves, sliced

2 Tbsp (30 mL) flour

1 bottle of red wine (750 mL),
preferably Beaujolais

4 sprigs of fresh thyme

8 cups (2 L) chicken stock

3 bay leaves

¼ cup (60 mL) unsalted butter

2 cups (500 mL) small white button mushrooms, left whole

sea salt and freshly ground pepper

Melt the butter in heavy-bottomed casserole and add the bacon. Cook over medium heat until bacon is crisp, drain on paper towels and place into a large bowl.

Season the chicken pieces with salt and pepper and cook them in the bacon drippings until they are golden brown. Transfer to the bowl with the bacon. Add the onions, carrot and celery root to the pan and cook slowly on medium heat, stirring from time to time, until the onion is translucent. Add the garlic, then stir in the flour and let cook for 3 to 5 minutes. Add the chicken, bacon, red wine, thyme and enough chicken stock to cover the chicken. Bring to a boil, reduce heat and cook, partially covered, for 45 minutes to 1 hour or until the chicken is tender.

Meanwhile, melt the remaining butter in a small pan and sauté the mushrooms until golden. Season them lightly with salt and pepper, then add to the chicken. To serve, ladle some of the sauce into a saucepan and reduce over high heat until thick and glossy.

Serve with the chicken and sauce over hot buttered noodles.

This classic French dish is a rich, slowly cooked chicken and herbs stewed with red wine. Using an older bird brings a richer flavour.

Tempura

Although indulging in fried food is always tempting, it seems especially so in winter. And if you are going to break your diet, better to do it at home where at least you can use fresh, good quality oil and ingredients. Batter-laced deep-frying is a Portuguese method of cooking that was introduced to Japan by missionaries during the 16th century. It became very popular, and by the 17th century, Tokyo street vendors were selling tempura using fish freshly caught in Tokyo Bay that was fried in sesame oil. Traditionally, the Japanese mix their tempura batter with chopsticks, ensuring that it is never over-mixed.

peanut oil

1 egg, beaten

1 cup (250 mL) cold beer

2 Tbsp (30 mL) dry white wine

½ cup (125 mL) flour

¼ cup (60 mL) rice flour

¼ cup (60 mL) corn starch

variety of vegetables and seafood, cut into bite-sized pieces

Heat peanut oil in a pan or deep fryer until temperature is 375° F (190° C). Combine egg, beer and white wine in a small bowl. In another bowl, combine flour, rice flour and cornstarch. Add liquid to dry mixture and very lightly mix together. The batter should look lumpy. Dip vegetables and seafood in tempura batter and fry in small batches until golden and crispy.

Tip

Keys to tasty, crispy tempura are a very light mixing of the batter—lumps are GOOD—and using an ice cold liquid, preferably one that is carbonated. To avoid greasy, soggy tempura, it is important to maintain the proper temperature of the oil, so it's best to have a thermometer on hand.

Tip

For deep-frying, peanut oil should be 2 to 3 inches (5 to 7.5 cm) deep or use deep fryer according to the manufacturer's directions.

The word tempura *comes from the Latin* ad tempora cuaresmae, *meaning "in the time of Lent." As good Catholics, the Portuguese missionaries substituted fish for meat at this time of the year, and batter-frying was a popular presentation.*

Balsamic-glazed Root Vegetables

Serves 4

Because of their long shelf life, root vegetables are important winter food. The term "root vegetable" is a general collective term that has come to include all vegetables, from a variety of families, that grow underground; for example, potatoes, carrots, onions, rutabagas and beets. Root vegetables were an important food source for Ontario's early settlers, providing vital nourishment for families through long winters. These vegetables were easy to grow, they kept well for extended periods of time and were filling, dense with carbohydrates. Even today, when many exotic, imported vegetables are available in Ontario's grocery stores, root vegetables remain staples for the same reasons they benefited our ancestors.

Root vegetables

1 lb (500 g) baby potatoes, a variety if possible, washed and halved or quartered, depending on size

2 medium parsnips, peeled and quartered lengthwise, then halved

1 medium yam, halved then sliced ¼ inch (.5 cm) thick

1 small beet, washed and quartered with skin on

1 large carrot, peeled and quartered lengthwise, then halved

1 bulb garlic, broken into cloves, peeled and left whole

1 small yellow onion, peeled and quartered

Marinade

¼ cup (60 mL) balsamic vinegar

¼ cup (60 mL) extra virgin olive oil or melted butter

2 Tbsp (30 mL) honey

¼ cup (60 mL) fresh parsley, finely chopped

sea salt and freshly ground pepper to taste

2 sprigs fresh thyme

2 sprigs fresh rosemary

Preheat oven to 375° F (190° C). Combine first four ingredients of the marinade and set aside.

Place the vegetables into a large mixing bowl. Pour the prepared marinade over top, season with salt and pepper and toss to coat. Place into 13 x 9-inch (33 x 23 cm) pan and assemble the rosemary and thyme sprigs on top. Roast uncovered, turning once or twice, for about 45 minutes or until the edges are golden brown and when pierced easily with a knife. Toss with fresh parsley and serve as a side dish.

Balsamic vinegar is an aged reduction sauce that originates in the Modena region of Italy. The best balsamic vinegar is aged a long time, comes in very small bottle and is very expensive. Instead, try a cheaper variety, but not the cheapest—it's most likely red vinegar and brown sugar or caramel.

Brandied Seville Marmalade with Lemon and Ginger

Makes 4 x 1 cup (250 mL) jars

Closely related to the Bergamot orange, which is used to flavour Earl Grey tea, the Seville orange is a species of bitter orange *(Citrus aurantium)* that originated in Vietnam. Inedible fresh, the Seville orange is prized for making marmalades, compotes and liqueurs, and it is the traditional ingredient in duck a l'orange. Because it was the Spaniards who first introduced this orange to the New World, it became associated with the famous Spanish city of Seville, where many of the streets are lined with Seville orange trees. In Ontario, you will find Seville oranges in your local grocers, usually for two to three weeks sometime from December to February. Making jams and marmalades is a wonderful way to occupy your time and lift your spirits during these cold winter months.

2 lbs (1 kg) Seville oranges (about 6) halved crosswise

2 lemons, halved crosswise

⅔ cup (150 mL) candied ginger, thinly sliced

water

sugar

⅓ cup (75 mL) brandy, optional

Place a 12-inch (30 cm) square of dampened cheesecloth in a bowl. Squeeze juice from Seville oranges and lemons into cheesecloth-lined bowl; using spoon or grapefruit knife, scoop seeds and pulp into bowl and tightly tie cheesecloth. Strain juice.

With a sharp knife, thinly slice orange and lemon peel. Combine the peel, candied ginger with the juice in a large measuring cup. Add an equal amount of water and pour into a large, heavy-bottomed pot. Place the pulp-seed bag into pot and bring to a boil over high heat. Reduce heat; cook gently uncovered, stirring occasionally, for about 2 hours until peel is tender and mixture is reduced. If desired, cover and let stand refrigerated at this stage.

Squeeze out the liquid from the cheesecloth bag before discarding. (If the bag is too hot to handle, let it cool a little.) Measure the remaining cooked peel and liquid together and place in a clean pot. Stir in an equal amount of sugar. Bring to a rapid boil, stirring often until marmalade thickens (see Wrinkle Test, next page). Remove from heat and skim off foam. Add brandy and stir marmalade continuously for 5 minutes to ensure the rind is evenly dispersed. Ladle into hot, sterilized jars to within ¼ inch (6 mm) of top rim. Wipe jar rim and apply lids and rings until fingertip tight; do not overtighten. Process jars in a boiling water canner for 5 minutes. Let rest at room temperature until set.

Wrinkle Test

Remove marmalade from heat, place a spoonful of marmalade on a plate that has been chilled in the freezer and return it to chill for 1 minute. To test, push your finger into the marmalade on the chilled plate; it will form a wrinkle when the right consistency has been reached. If marmalade gel is insufficient, return mixture to a rolling boil and test again.

Tip

For a unique and interesting houseplant try planting a few seeds from your Seville oranges. Though they are unlikely to fruit indoors, they are attractive, bushy plants that grow well in a sunny window and make lovely patio specimens if moved outdoors for the summer.

Molasses Bran Muffins

Makes 12 muffins

Molasses was the most common household sweetener up until the late 19th century because of the high cost of refined sugar. The cost was why so many historical recipes such as ginger cookies and cakes, shoofly pie, baked beans and taffy feature molasses and are still common today. There are three types of molasses on the market: unsulphured, sulphured and blackstrap. Unsulphured molasses is the highest quality and most pure molasses. Blackstrap molasses, which should also be unsulphured, is an excellent source of iron and is high in calcium and copper. Sulphured molasses should be avoided. The Redpath Sugar Company, a fixture on the Toronto waterfront for over 75 years, produces molasses in Ontario from imported sugar cane or domestically grown sugar beets. The Redpath label is Canada's oldest continuously used logo for a food company.

1¼ cups (310 mL) bran cereal

1½ cups (375 mL) buttermilk

¾ cup (175 mL) molasses

½ cup (125 mL) canola or sunflower oil

1 egg, beaten

⅔ cup (150 mL) pitted dates, chopped

1¾ cups (435 mL) flour

1 Tbsp (15 mL) baking powder

1 tsp (5 mL) baking soda

pinch of salt

Preheat oven to 400° F (200° C) and spray a muffin tin with nonstick spray. Set aside.

In a bowl, mix the cereal and buttermilk and let stand for 5 minutes. Add the molasses, oil and egg, and stir to combine. Stir in the dates. Set aside.

In another bowl, sift together the dry ingredients. Fold the dry into the wet until just combined, then fill each muffin tin almost full with batter.

Bake for 12 to 15 minutes or until the tops of the muffins spring back with light pressure. Allow to cool for 5 minutes and then remove from pan.

Tip

Buttermilk and sour milk are often used interchangeably in recipes. To make your own sour milk, put 2 to 3 tsp (5 to 10 mL) of lemon juice or vinegar in a measuring cup and add enough milk for 1 cup (250 mL) of liquid. Let the mixture sit for about 10 minutes.

About 10 percent of all sugar in Canada comes from sugar beets, and though they were originally grown in Ontario, the prairie provinces now produce all the sugar beets that are grown.

Sunflower Granola

A perfect start to a cold, dark winter morning, granola first became popular in the 1960s with the hippie movement. Its origins go back a bit farther, though, to Dr. John Harvey Kellogg, who in the 1870s developed the concoction as part of the Seventh Day Adventist vegetarian and whole-grain based diet at Battle Creek Sanitarium. There is no right or wrong way to make granola, and it can include many ingredients. The sunflower seed featured in this granola is typical of the seeds that have been grown in Ontario for several decades for both human consumption and birdseed. Sunflower seeds are ready to harvest in Ontario from September to mid-October.

4 cups (1 L) old-fashioned oats (not quick)

1 cup (250 mL) unsweetened, shredded coconut

1 cup (250 mL) dried fruit of choice: blueberries, cherries, sliced apricots, etc.

1 cup (250 mL) pumpkin seeds

1½ cups (375 mL) sunflower seeds

½ cup (125 mL) sesame seeds

1 cup (250 mL) wheat germ

1 cup (250 mL) chopped almonds

½ cup (125 mL) chopped cashews

⅔ cup (150 mL) maple syrup

1 tsp (5 mL) pure vanilla extract

½ tsp (2 mL) salt

¼ cup (60 mL) sunflower oil

Preheat oven to 325° F (160° C). Place all ingredients in a large bowl and mix well. Spread on a baking sheet and bake for 15 minutes. Stir and bake 10 more minutes. Stir again and bake 5 to 10 minutes more until golden brown. Cool and store in an airtight container for up to a month.

Tip
Sprinkle granola over your favourite cereal or yogurt, or simply enjoy with milk. You can also eat it plain by the handful, or you can freeze it for use at another time.

Preserved Lemons

Although they are available all year, lemons (*Citrus limon*) and other citrus fruit peak during winter, providing a welcome sunny break when it is cold and snowy outside. Lemons are among the chef's arsenal of "secret ingredients": nine times out of ten, when something is missing from a concoction, a squeeze of lemon juice inevitably does the trick. Preserved lemons can be used in all the ways you use fresh lemon juice, yet they also offer a mysterious meatiness the juice just can't deliver. Lemons are actually a cultivated hybrid of the citron and mandarin, believed to have first been used in central India.

8 lemons, organic highly recommended

1 cup (250 mL) kosher salt

2 to 4 cups (500 mL to 1 L) fresh lemon juice, enough to cover the lemons

Optional Spices

2 bay leaves

4 coriander seeds

4 black peppercorns

1 cinnamon stick

2 whole cloves

Make 2 cuts in lemons, from the top to within ½ inch (1 cm) of the bottom, almost quartering them but not going all the way through. Pack salt into each lemon and reshape.

Place 1 tablespoon (15 mL) salt on the bottom of two 4-cup (2 x 1 L) preserving jars. Push lemons into the jars and squish them down, adding more salt and spices, if you are using, between each layer of lemon, until all the salt is used. Fill the remaining space in the jars with fresh lemon juice to approximately ¾ inch (2 cm) from top of jars, being sure lemons are completely covered.

Seal and store in a cool, dark part of your pantry for 4 weeks, giving the jars a little shake every once in a while. After 4 weeks, the lemons are ready to use. Remove them from the jars as needed. They can be stored in a cool, dark pantry, or in the refrigerator, if you prefer, for up to 6 months.

Variation
Try preserving a mixture of limes and lemons.

Angel Food Cake with Passion Fruit Sauce

Serves 6 to 8

Angel food cake is the quintessential "recovery from the holiday-binge" dessert! This fat-free cake is soft, airy and light. It is difficult to pin down its origin, but it likely first appeared in the late 19th century. Some people attribute angel food cake to the Pennsylvania Dutch, mainly because of their history of using special moulds to form festive cakes. Angel food cake is rare among desserts in that it is fat-free—in fact, it must be kept completely away from oils or fats (including stray bits of egg yolk) in order to achieve its characteristic spongy lightness. Before starting, it is vital that all your utensils and bowls be squeaky clean.

1 cup (250 mL) sifted cake flour

1½ cups (375 mL) berry sugar, divided into two ¾-cup (175 mL) portions

¼ tsp (1 mL) sea salt

12 egg whites

1½ tsp (8 mL) vanilla or almond extract

¼ cup (60 mL) warm water

1½ tsp (8 mL) cream of tartar

Preheat oven at 375° F (190° C). Sift the flour, half of the sugar and salt, repeat 3 times and set aside. In an electric mixer, beat egg whites, vanilla or almond extract and water with cream of tartar at medium-high speed until foamy. Slowly sift in the remaining sugar, beating until you have medium-firm peaks.

Sift about ½ cup (125 mL) of the flour mixture over whites and gently fold just until flour disappears. Repeat, folding in remaining flour mixture ½ cup (125 mL) at a time. Pour batter into an ungreased 10-inch (25 cm) angel food pan. Bake until cake springs back when lightly touched, about 30 to 40 minutes. Invert pan on a cooling rack or on the neck of a bottle in order to maintain as much volume or height of the cake as possible. Cool completely and serve with passion fruit sauce.

For the passion fruit sauce, cut the fresh fruit in half and spoon out pulp. Bring the apple juice and sugar to a boil in a saucepan and cook over medium heat for about 15 minutes or until thick and syrupy. Add the passion fruit pulp and lemon juice and boil for another 3 minutes and remove from heat. Pour the sauce into a clean jar and refrigerate up to a week.

In Ontario, passion flower (Passiflora *spp.*) is an annual or tender perennial woody climber that produces spectacular flowers, but the fruit isn't very tasty. Look for tropically grown passion fruit in stores in late fall and early winter.

Passion Fruit Sauce

1 cup (250 mL) fresh passion fruit pulp, from about 6 passion fruit

⅓ cup (75 mL) unsweetened apple juice

1 cup (250 mL) sugar

juice of ½ lemon

INDEX